TAUNTON'S GETTING STARTED IN WOODWORKING™

Projects for Your Shop

Projects for Your Shop

Building Your
Own Workshop
Essentials

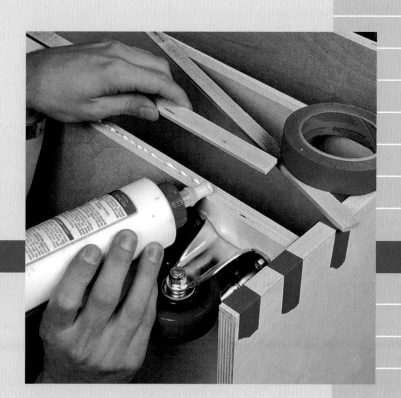

Matthew Teague

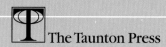
The Taunton Press

The Taunton Press, Inc., 63 South Main Street, PO Box 5506, Newtown, CT 06470-5506

The Taunton Press
Inspiration for hands-on living®

e-mail: tp@taunton.com

Editor: Jennifer Renjilian Morris
Interior design: Barbara Balch
Layout: Barbara Balch
Illustrator: Chuck Lockhart
Photographer: Matthew Teague

Taunton's Getting Started in Woodworking™ is a trademark of The Taunton Press, Inc.,
registered in the U.S. Patent and Trademark Office.

Library of Congress Cataloging-in-Publication Data
Teague, Matthew.
  Projects for your shop : building your own workshop essentials / Matthew Teague.
      p. cm. -- (Taunton's getting started in woodworking)
  Includes index.
  ISBN 1-56158-689-7
  1. Workshops--Equipment and supplies--Design and construction. 2. Woodwork--Equipment and
supplies--Design and construction. I. Title. II. Series.
  TT152.T43 2005
  684'.08--dc22
                            2005009594

Printed in the United States of America
10 9 8 7 6 5 4 3 2 1

The following manufacturers/names appearing in *Projects for Your Shop* are trademarks: Bench Dog
Tools®, Watco®

ABOUT YOUR SAFETY

Working with wood is inherently dangerous. Using hand or power tools improperly or ignoring safety practices can lead to permanent injury or even death. Don't try to perform operations you learn about here (or elsewhere) unless you're certain they are safe for you. If something about an operation doesn't feel right, don't do it. Look for another way. We want you to enjoy the craft, so please keep safety foremost in your mind whenever you're in the shop.

Acknowledgments

This book is for my father, who kept handing me sticks and knives, and my mother, who allowed it.

This book is the product of a great many hands. First and foremost, this book would not have happened without Helen Albert, whose trust and guidance helped develop this book, and Jennifer Renjilian Morris, whose deft editing pen (and calculator) made sense of my messes and kept this book on schedule. Wendi Mijal provided excellent art direction for photographs, even from a thousand miles away. Julie Hamilton, Kathleen Williams, Jenny Peters, and the host of people at Taunton whose hands have touched this book—none of whom are too professional to be human—are a pleasure and honor to work with. I'm proud to have my work alongside Chuck Lockhart's fine illustrations and Barbara Balch's handsome layout.

I'd also like to thank Tim Schreiner and Bob Goodfellow—both of whom taught me more than they know—as well as the staff at *Fine Woodworking*. My years at that magazine allowed me to learn more than one craft. Michael Pekovich and John White were especially fine woodworking instructors, whether they knew it or not.

There is also a cast of craftsmen across the country with whom I worked at *Fine Woodworking*, and I can't think of one who didn't teach me something I didn't know—much of which is in this book. A few were kind enough to pick up the phone to lend guidance as I wrote this book: Scott Gibson, Andy Rae, Lonnie Bird, Mario Rodriguez, Lon Schleining, Gary Rogowski, Curtis Buchanan, and Tom Lie-Nielsen. Thanks to all of you.

Chad Corley at Delta/Porter-Cable, Jason Felder at Bosch Power Tools, and Warren Weber at Bench Dog Tools were always quick to loan out tools and provide assistance along the way.

I was also lucky enough to be able to enlist the work of my family on this book. My father and brother John helped me out of the pinches that couldn't be managed with two hands alone.

Most of all, thanks to my wife, Sarah, whose love, encouragement, and constant smile keep me going.

Contents

Introduction

When I started woodworking as a kid, my father kept all his tools in the laundry room. He had a circular saw, a jigsaw, chisels, and screwdrivers, even a small lathe and a small bandsaw. To use them, usually on Saturday afternoons, we'd move them out to the back deck and run an extension cord through the kitchen window. It wasn't elaborate, but it was a good place to learn the basics. And we spent hours there—sweating in the summer and wearing long johns in the winter. Twenty years later, my

one-car garage is what many would still consider a modest workshop. But it's more than enough for me.

Whether you're working on your back porch or in an expansive basement shop, chances are you're there for the same reasons I am: You enjoy the peace and quiet, the satisfaction of doing it yourself, and the pride that comes from building something you know will be handed down from your children to theirs.

Whatever your shop space, you'll enjoy your time there a lot more if it has efficient workstations and smart organization. Efficiency will turn your shop into an inspiring space, where work progresses smoothly and hours pass by without your noticing. I hope this book will be a step in that direction for you.

The projects in this book are no-nonsense, straightforward pieces designed to improve both your workshop and your woodworking skills. When learning to build a set of sawhorses, you'll become familiar with a circular saw. And as you build a workbench, you'll become more skilled with the circular saw and learn the ins and outs of a router and biscuit joiner as well. When you make a stand and outfeed tables for your tablesaw, you'll learn to join a case piece using biscuits—a task you'll encounter repeatedly as a woodworker. Building a router table, you'll learn another common method for building cases: using the tablesaw to cut dadoes and rabbets.

Not only will your skills grow, but your tool collection will grow as well. A dark table in the corner of your shop is not a tool, but a workbench with a vise and a bench stop is. Likewise, a benchtop tablesaw will cut wood, but its precision and usefulness multiply when you incorporate it into a smart workstation design.

Whether you're interested in building bookshelves around the house or framing up a shed out back, this book walks you through building the basic accessories you'll need to make your shop run as smoothly as any good tool. And working on your own shop is the best way to hone your woodworking skills. In

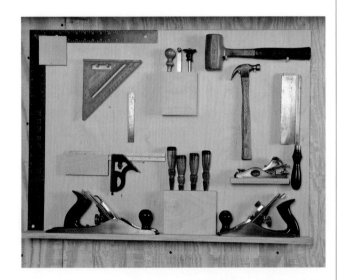

the process of outfitting your shop, you'll learn all the basics of woodworking. And if you make mistakes, you're making them on a 2x4 or a few dollars' worth of plywood instead of that antique board from a tree felled at your great-grandfather's house. If there's a misaligned screw or an unfaired edge, hey, it's just shop stuff—before long it'll be covered in sawdust anyway. The important thing is that you're learning and enjoying yourself.

Tools and Materials

Woodworkers are often guilty when it comes to overspending on tools. I'm guilty myself. But truth be told, it's just not necessary.

You can build just about anything with the minimal set of tools used in this book: a set of hand tools, a few handheld power tools, and your first stationary tool, a benchtop table saw. Chances are, you already have a few of these tools for projects around the house. Or maybe you're an experienced woodworker and have most of these tools already. In that case, this book will give you sound ideas for fine-tuning the workstations in your shop. Either way, the tool set outlined in this chapter is the core of any efficient workshop, and it's a collection worth putting together.

You'll also need minimal materials for these projects, and they're affordable. Most of these projects call for plywood or other sheet goods, and there are many different styles to choose from. You'll also be using solid wood for edging projects, building face frames for cabinets, and occasional small tasks where plywood is inappropriate. Aside from that, you'll need only a few small hardware items, like hinges and T-handles, most of which can be purchased at the local hardware store. In a few instances, you'll want to mail-order specialty items, like large bench bolts or a preglued benchtop, from woodworking catalogs or websites. Add a few drywall screws, a bottle of glue, and a box of nails, and you're ready to go.

After building these projects, both your workshop and your techniques will be honed. With your newfound skills and confidence, you'll be ready to move on to less-basic tools and a larger variety of materials.

Hand Tools

To get started, you'll need a good set of hand tools, including tools for marking and measuring, planing edges smooth, and chiseling. While these tools are necessary for the projects in this book, they're also the tools you'll find most handy around the shop, no matter what you're building. Learning to use hand tools properly is a good starting point for the beginning woodworker, but it's also a good way for seasoned woodworkers to brush up on the most basic skills. You'll want to look for hand tools that are comfortable to your hands and made of high-quality steel, but there's no reason to buy top-of-the-line tools. Antique hand tools that you've inherited or found at

garage sales are often quality tools that just need a little cleaning and tuning up. In many cases, the older tools are better and more affordable than what you can buy at the hardware store. Whatever you choose, these tools will be the cornerstone for your tool collection.

Marking and measuring tools

For marking, all you really need is a good pencil. You'll also want a marking gauge, which you'll use to mark an exact distance from the edge of a board to a point on that board. You might also want an awl to mark nail holes.

For measuring and laying out joinery, a combination square is a must. You'll frequently use it for laying out cut lines, but you'll also find yourself grabbing it for tasks ranging from setting the blade on your table saw to checking the thickness of a piece of

Rulers and squares A tape measure is good for starters, but you'll probably want a folding rule in time. A combination square is a constant companion in the shop. Though not absolutely necessary, a tri-square comes in handy for less exacting tasks.

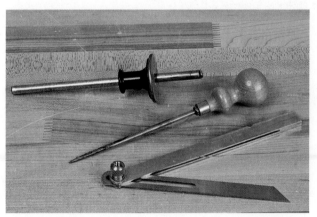

Marking tools A bevel gauge (bottom) allows you to dial in the right angle, an awl (middle) is good for starting holes before drilling, and a marking gauge (top) allows you to mark lines parallel to an edge.

plywood. You'll also want to pick up a good tape measure or a cabinetmaker's folding rule. I usually prefer the folding rule because the measurements are more precise and because a portion of it is retractable—allowing you to measure inside a case piece—but either will work. In some situations, you'll find a tri-square, framing square, and a bevel gauge helpful, but you can probably get by without them.

Handplanes

You'll want two different planes for smoothing the surfaces and edges of wood: a small block plane for beveling edges and smoothing over short lengths, and either a #4 smoothing plane or a #5 jack plane for smoothing larger surfaces and flattening edges. Most woodworkers suggest a #4 as a first plane, and it works just fine, but I went for years with nothing but a good #5. In a pinch, it can do just about anything, from beveling edges to flattening tabletops.

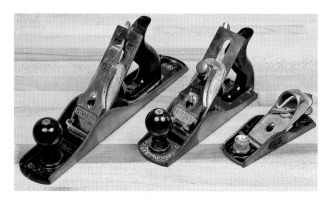

You'll need at least two planes A large #4 or #5 plane is good for smoothing edges and surfaces, and a block plane excels at trimming and beveling edges.

Chisels

You can spend as much or as little as you want on chisels, all based on the quality of the steel used. Moderately priced chisels usually hold a good edge and are more than sufficient. I have a $35 set of four chisels that handle any task I've ever asked of them. I also rely on a set of shorter, antique chisels with wooden handles. Whatever brand you choose, make sure the chisels fit your hands and feel comfortable. For the most flexibility, you'll want a few different widths—one each of ¼", ½", ¾", and 1".

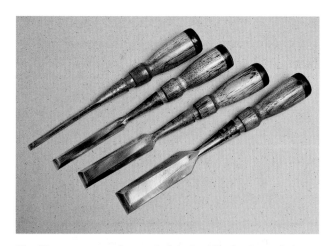

You'll want a good set of chisels Find a brand that feels comfortable in your hands and look for a set of four, ranging in size from ¼" to 1".

Handheld Power Tools

Y ou'll use the power tools featured in this book for pretty much anything you'll ever build. And if you own a house or have to repair the place you're renting, chances are you'll wind up buying most of these at some point anyway.

Drill/drivers

N o shop—or house, for that matter— should be without a cordless drill/driver. With a cordless drill/driver, you can drill holes and drive screws anywhere. Larger-voltage tools have more power but are heavier. You need at least a 9-volt drill/driver, but I'd suggest a 14-volt model. It's strong enough to drive screws into hardwoods and has a good battery life, but it's also light enough to keep from wearing your arm out. Anything over 14 volts gets heavy. It's usually best to buy a set or two of drill bits—pilot or brad-point bits for drilling holes up to ½" and a set of Forstner bits for boring larger holes.

Cordless drill/drivers are the best route A 14-volt drill/driver and two sets of bits—one for small holes and one for large—is all you need to get started.

Routers

W ith a router, you'll be able to mill dados and rabbets, cut profiled edges on boards, and perform a host of other woodworking tasks. Once you learn the basics of the tool, a router quickly becomes a go-to machine. I'd suggest buying a combo set, which comes with both a fixed and a plunge base. You'll want the plunge base for most handheld tasks and the fixed base to mount in a router table. The basic 1-hp machine will do all the tasks required in this book, but if you can spend a little more, opt for a machine with variable speeds, which you'll need if you ever want to make raised panels or use large bits to profile edges. Make sure you get a machine with a ½" collet and

Routers—fixed base or plunge The best option is to buy a set that offers one router with two different bases—a plunge base for handheld work and a fixed base for attaching to a router table.

use ½" bits whenever possible, because they're much safer than the smaller ¼" bits.

Circular saw

A circular saw comes in handy for cutting stock to length, and also for cutting large sheets of plywood to manageable size. Unless you're in a fully equipped shop in a large space, you're going to need a circular saw, but because you'll use it mostly for rough work, there's no reason to overspend.

Other tools

In addition to the tools already mentioned, you'll want a jigsaw for making curved cuts or cutting out the middle of a board.

A random-orbit sander—either 5" or 6" in diameter—will cut your sanding time dramatically. That said, you can get by with a good sanding block and a little elbow grease.

The one specialized tool I'd suggest is a biscuit joiner. The biscuit joiner is the secret of cabinetmakers everywhere. With it, you cut small divots into the edges of mating boards, then simply glue a football-shaped biscuit between the two. The result is a strong joint that can handle a lot of weight.

The power tools you'll need With a biscuit joiner, a circular saw, a jigsaw, and a random-orbit sander, you're on your way to a fully equipped shop.

You only need a basic model for this tool, so there's no need to overspend.

Stationary Machines

The only larger machine you'll need is a table saw. What you see in this book is a small benchtop saw. Though many benchtop saws come with stands that raise them to a proper working height and give them a larger footprint, they're named for their small size. They're small enough to be attached to a workbench, a sawhorse, or a table, then stored out of the way when not in use. Their capacity is smaller than some other models, so you'll want to keep your circular saw and cutting guide handy for ripping large sheet goods to size.

Benchtop saws are relatively inexpensive, and they're a good choice for someone just getting started in woodworking. If you're working around the house or building small pieces of furniture, a benchtop saw will become your quick friend, and it may well be the only tablesaw you'll ever need. You can buy a stand with the saw, but you'll get a lot more use by mounting your saw on a permanent base that provides stability and more outfeed support (see Tablesaw Workstation on pp. 56–89).

You may also decide that you want a drill press. There are a few occasions in this book when you could use one. But you can perform the same tasks with a drilling guide—they're not all that exact, but they are more than adequate for these purposes. They're also inexpensive.

A miter saw is the other tool you may want to consider. It makes cutting angles or cutting boards to length easy, but you can use either a circular saw or a tablesaw instead, depending on the situation.

An almost-stationary tool A benchtop saw doesn't have the heft of a larger stationary machine, but it'll do all you need and more, especially if it's installed in a proper workstation.

Materials

The materials needed for the projects in this book are among the most basic: plywood, 2x4s, 2x6s, a little bit of solid wood, and the glue, screws, nails, and hinges you'd use for most any project. You'll also need a few straightforward but uncommon items: a prefabricated benchtop, T-handles, and bench bolts, which you'll learn more about in the Workbench chapter on pp. 28–55.

Wood

Most of these projects are built using plywood. Plywood, even the nicer grades, is inexpensive compared to solid wood. But plywood is also more stable, meaning that, unlike solid wood, it expands and contracts very little with changes in humidity. You have a choice of thicknesses, ranging from ⅛" to ¾". For these reasons, plywood is a good choice for your first projects—and any shop projects. For a cleaner look, you can dress it up by applying a solid wood edge (see Router Table on pp. 90–121).

When it comes to sheet goods, you'll find dozens of products on the market. For this kind of work, you'll need to choose between interior pine plywood or hardwood plywood (like pine plywood but faced with birch, oak, or a similar hardwood veneer). I try to stay away from pine plywood, because it is often fraught with voids in the inner layers of the wood and uneven outer surfaces. A hardwood plywood like oak or birch is a better option, and only slightly more expensive. Throughout this book, I've opted for a slightly higher

Choosing solid wood Look for a species that matches the plywood you'll be pairing it with. Seen here are pine, oak, poplar, and maple, all of which are good choices. Use pine when wear and tear isn't a concern.

grade of plywood made of Baltic birch. I prefer it because the exposed edges of the plywood look nicer, but the slightly cheaper hardwood plywood at your local home center will work just as well.

You can also use medium-density fiberboard (MDF), a composite material that machines beautifully and is as stable as plywood. It's much less expensive, but it's quite heavy (especially if you're lugging around full 8' by 4' sheets of it). And unless you have good dust collection on all your tools, the dust it creates can wreak havoc on your sinuses. For those reasons, I try to stay away from it.

There are a few instances in which I recommend solid wood. Except for the projects involving 2x4s and 2x6s—which, in this book, are always pine or fir—you'll have to decide between a few options. I've used maple throughout the book, but oak or poplar would work just as well. Pine or fir works also, but you won't want to use it in cases where you need a dense, hard surface, like around the workbench. I'd suggest picking a hardwood that matches the color of your plywood. Because I've used Baltic birch throughout, the pale color of maple matches nicely.

Choosing sheet goods From the bottom to the top: MDF, pine plywood, birch plywood, oak plywood, and Baltic birch plywood.

WORK SMART

When using MDF, make sure you seal all the surfaces with at least one coat of finish—if moisture gets to the surface, the compressed materials expand, leaving an uneven surface.

Other materials

As for the smaller supplies you'll need, most can be purchased at the local hardware store or home center. You can buy nails and screws as you need them, but I'd suggest going out and buying a few boxes of both finish nails and coarse-thread drywall screws in a few different sizes. You'll use them for most projects you build, so you'll always need them. You'll also need hinges, clamps, sandpaper, and a few specialty items.

For glues, you'll mostly use a woodworking grade of plain old yellow glue, but get some 5-minute epoxy, too, for quick fixes.

For sanding, use paper-backed sandpaper for most tasks, but choose automotive-grade cloth-backed paper for sanding finishes. Most shop furniture is fine without any finish at all, but in some cases you'll apply wax, shellac, or polyurethane.

Keeping it together For simple projects, you'll need only a woodworker's grade of yellow glue and, for quick fixes, a 5-minute epoxy.

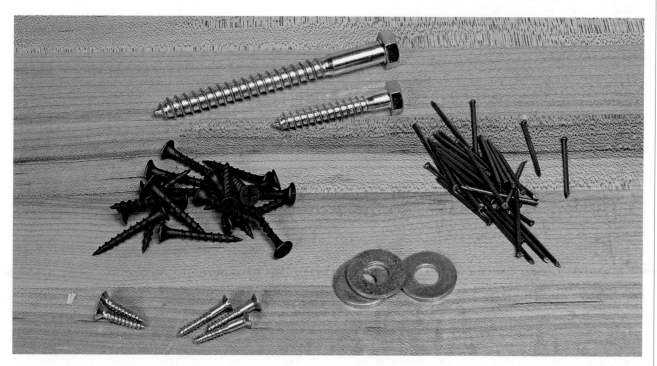

A surer fastener Finish nails (right), drywall screws (left), large lag screws (top), and washers (bottom, center) will secure the bulk of your work. Brass and steel wood screws (lower left) are used for smaller hinges and hardware.

Sawhorses

Sawhorses have been around about as long as people have been cutting boards, and they're as useful now as ever. Whether you use them for assembling large cabinets, gluing up tabletops, ripping plywood, or crosscutting stock to length, sawhorses support lumber to keep your work safer and easier to manage. When you're working solo, they're a great helping hand. No matter how well equipped your shop, you won't leave sawhorses sitting unused for long. These light and versatile tools are one of the first pieces you'll want to build for your shop.

The mobility of a sawhorse is one of its great perks. Lay a piece of plywood over a pair of horses, and you've got a makeshift workbench that is more mobile than the heavy bench you work on every day. This ability to relocate your workspace quickly is great in small shops or in garage shops that share room with the family car. But mobility is a must for work outside the shop. If you're installing shelving in your living room or repairing the bathroom vanity, a pair of sawhorses allows you to work on site.

Depending on the work at hand, and if it's a nice, clear day, you're as likely to find me working in the driveway on sawhorses as you are at the workbench in my shop. I also use them for building sheds, potting benches, and various other garden structures in the yard. A sturdy sawhorse, like the shopmade version built in this chapter, also comes in handy as a stepladder.

What You'll Learn

- **Ripping and crosscutting with a circular saw**
- **Countersinking and driving screws**
- **Using a bevel gauge to mark out angled cuts**

Drive smart Use your own weight or a clamp to hold the top in place as you countersink screws to secure the top. Here, a 2x6 top creates a larger work surface.

I built my first sawhorses about 15 years ago, and though I've added a few new boards to replace the sacrificial tops, they're still as stable as ever. And they've lived much of their life outside—for the last three years they've held up a canoe behind my shop. After all that, they've stayed rock solid, even though they are held together with only glue and screws.

These sawhorses are a slight improvement on those I've relied on for many years. Because the tops of sawhorses are often cut up from circular saws, routers, and various other tools, this sawhorse features a top that can be renewed by simply removing a few screws and replacing the sacrificial top board. The sawhorses seen in this chapter feature a versatile 2x4 top, but the same design works with either a 2x6 or 2x8 on the top (see the 2x6 top in the photo at right). A wider top board gives you a wider worksurface, turning even a lone horse into a small, mobile workbench.

Building these horses takes only a circular saw, a drill, and a handful of drywall screws. If you've already got a miter saw, you can save a little time by making all the 15° cuts on it, but a circular saw works just fine. And building a pair of these sawhorses with a circular saw takes only about two hours.

In the course of building these sawhorses, you'll learn safe methods for using a circular saw as well as how to drive screws without any fear of splitting boards. You'll also learn to mark out various angles with a bevel gauge. If you have little experience in woodworking, building sawhorses is a good way to start learning. If you're more experienced, it might just be time to replace the wobbly sawhorses that sit in the corner of almost every shop.

Build Your Own Sawhorse

This design is built quickly using only 2x4s, a little plywood, and drywall screws. For insurance, you can add glue, but be sure to leave the top unglued so you can replace it in the future.

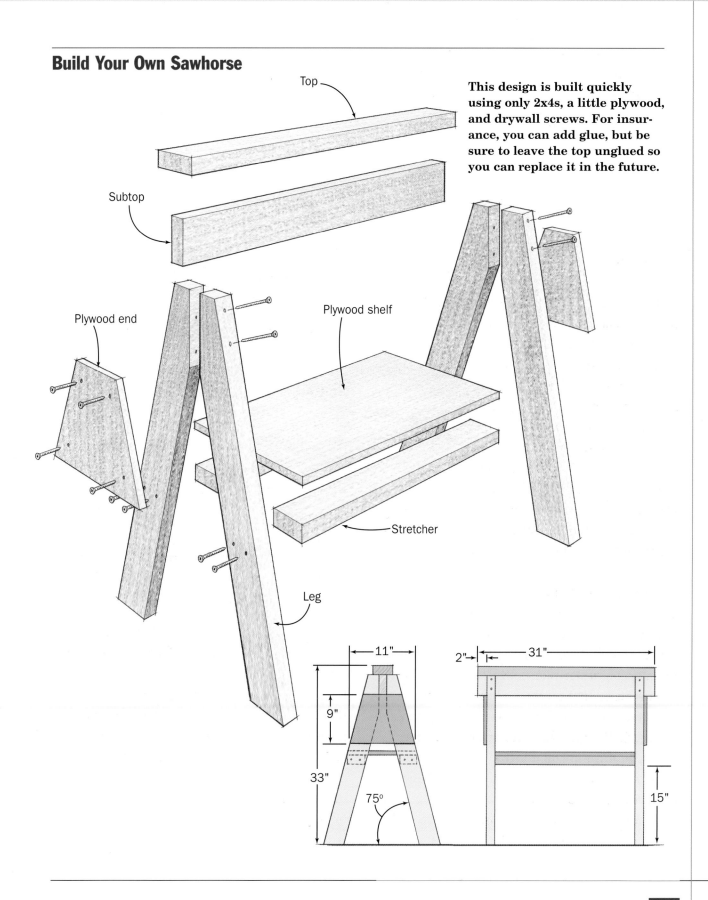

Top

Subtop

Plywood end

Plywood shelf

Stretcher

Leg

11"

9"

33"

75°

2"

31"

15"

Sawhorses

Your first sawhorses should be about waist high—these stand about 33" tall when complete—but you may want to build other heights in the future. A low set of horses, about 15" to 20" high, comes in handy for assembling large case goods, while horses about 40" high make great worktables for routing, handplaning, and other operations done standing upright. For other sawhorse designs, see "Design Options" on pp. 26–27.

MATERIALS

Quantity	Part	Actual Size	What to Buy
1	Top	1½" x 3½" x 31"	2x4
1	Subtop	1½" x 3½" x 31"	2x4
2	End braces	¾" x 9" x 8"	Plywood
1	Shelf	¾" x 13" x 24"	Plywood
2	Stretchers	1½" x 3½" x 24"	2x4
4	Legs	1½" x 3½" x 33"	2x4
	Ledge (optional)		Narrow strips of scrap wood or lengths of ¼" plywood work well as a ledge around the shelf.
1 box	Drywall screws	3"	
1 box	Drywall screws	2½"	
1 box	Drywall screws	1½"	

Buying Materials

The materials needed for this project can be found at any home center. When picking lumber, look for straight boards without any bend. To figure out if a board is straight, sight down one edge—you can easily see a curve when you look along the board's length. A half sheet of plywood is more than enough to build a pair of horses. A 2x4 top seems to make the handiest top for this sawhorse, but the design can just as easily accept a 2x6 or even a 2x8.

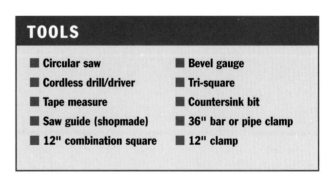

TOOLS

- Circular saw
- Cordless drill/driver
- Tape measure
- Saw guide (shopmade)
- 12" combination square
- Bevel gauge
- Tri-square
- Countersink bit
- 36" bar or pipe clamp
- 12" clamp

Cut the Legs to Length

When you've determined the height of your sawhorse, you need to cut the four legs to length and cut 15° angles on each end. It's easiest to cut the legs to rough length, then gang-cut the angles all at once. If you're without a decent worksurface, you can simply set the legs on scrap 2x4s or on 2" rigid foam and cut them right on the floor.

1. Cut the legs to rough length with a circular saw, as shown in photo A.

2. Stagger the legs and clamp them together edge to edge. Then clamp the whole assembly down to a flat worksurface. Make sure to use two clamps to secure them—one clamp will simply act as a pivot.

3. Once the boards are secure, set the bevel gauge for a 15° angle. To set your bevel gauge, mark out 15° from a tri-square on a scrap board, then transfer the angle to your

Cut to rough length When cutting stock to rough length, make sure it's clamped in place and keep both hands on the saw. Allow offcuts to fall freely so that they won't bind the blade.

bevel gauge and lock it in place, as shown in photos B and C. If the bevel gauge is not at 15° exactly, don't worry about it—what matters is that your angles are all the same. You can use a tri-square to set out the angle on the

Determine the angle Use a tri-square on a scrap board or worksurface to mark out a 15° angle. Transfer the angle to a bevel gauge and use that to mark throughout the project.

Set the bevel gauge Transfer the angle from the tri-square to the bevel gauge. Be sure to tighten the bevel gauge well so that it won't get knocked out of place.

Mark out the angle Clamp the legs together and transfer the angle from the bevel gauge.

Extend the angle Use a long ruler or straightedge to continue the angled line.

legs, but I find marking out to be a lot easier with a bevel gauge, and you can keep the gauge set at 15° to use later in the project.

4. Use the bevel gauge to mark one end of one leg with the angle, as shown in photo D. Then use a straightedge to extend the angle mark across the other three legs, as shown in photo E.

5. Cut the angle across all four legs at once using a circular saw. With all four legs clamped together, it's like you're cutting a single board. To ensure that you cut a consistent angle and stay to the line, it's best to use a cutting guide to guide your circular saw, as shown in photo F. For more on making a cutting guide, see "A Shopmade Cutting Guide" on the facing page.

Cut the angled ends Using a circular saw guide guarantees a straight cut. After cutting, leave the legs clamped together and repeat the same process on the other end.

> **WORK SMART**
>
> When crosscutting numerous lengths of lumber to the same size, clamp them all together and cut them in a single pass.

6. With the legs still clamped together, you'll cut the other ends so the clamped-up legs form the shape of a parallelogram. Begin by measuring out the length on one leg—in this case, 33"—and adding another clamp across that end of the legs. Then draw in the angle using the same marking method you used to mark the first cut. Repeat the same cutting process as above, cutting all the legs in one pass.

A straightedge clamped in place allows you to cut a crisp line. It comes in handy for cutting large sheets of plywood to size. To make one, use ¼" plywood as the base and thicker plywood on the top as the guide. Just make sure the plywood used for the guide isn't so thick that it interferes with the saw casing when you cut. Once the base and guide are attached, saw through the base with the foot of your saw against the straight-edge on the guide. Now, the edge of the guide's base will denote exactly the point where the blade cuts. The small guide seen here can be made in various lengths to accommodate different lengths of lumber.

Circular Saw Guide

A cutting guide is quickly made from scrap plywood around the shop. The base of the circular saw rides against the 3/4" plywood, and the blade runs against the thinner ply below.

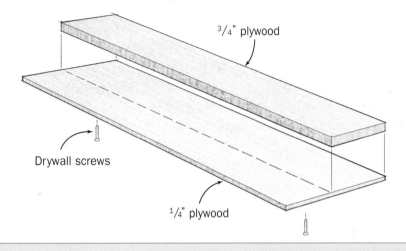

3/4" plywood

Drywall screws

¼" plywood

To use the guide, line up the edge of the guide's base with the line you're cutting and clamp it in place. To cut, butt the base of the saw against the straightedge and keep it there throughout the cut.

Cut the Legs to Accept the Top

One advantage of this design is that you don't have to cut a ridge on the legs to hold the top in place. Instead, you make angled cuts on the legs so that you can screw them directly to a subtop that is perpendicular to the floor.

1. With the base of a combination square flush against the outer edge of the leg, mark a line 2" in from the outside edge of the leg, as shown in photo G.

G

Measure in from the edge of the leg Use a combination square to mark the legs 2" in.

Because it's used for everything from building houses to putting up fences to making kitchen cabinets, a circular saw is among the first power tools a woodworker buys. It's a relatively simple tool, but any time you work with a sharp, spinning blade, there are some risks. As long as you understand those risks and know how to avoid them, there's no reason a circular saw can't be used safely.

Kickback is the biggest danger you'll encounter with a circular saw. Kickback is when a blade binds in the cut and the saw kicks back toward you. But you can take measures to prevent it.

1. Make sure you're using a good-quality blade. A moderately priced, carbide-toothed blade rated for general-purpose work should handle most situations.

2. Every time you make a cut, adjust the cutting depth to match your workpiece. Make sure the blade clears the material but doesn't protrude more than ⅛" on the underside.

3. Make sure the offcut can fall freely to the floor without binding on the blade, and always cut in a straight line. Clamp the work in place, then follow a line, keeping both hands on the saw as shown in photo A. If getting a square cut is important, use a tri-square to keep cuts straight, as shown in photo B, but only if you're sure the work is well secured.

4. When you're cutting on sawhorses, make your cut perpendicular to the tops of the sawhorses, rather than parallel to them, so that both sides of the stock are supported throughout the cut, as shown in photo C. If you cut parallel to the tops on the sawhorses, the weight of the saw can cause the stock to bind and create a kickback.

Mark a line to the opposite edge **Hold the combination square against the end of the leg and draw a line to the inside edge of the leg.**

2. Set a combination square on the end of the leg at the mark you made in step 1. Mark a line from that mark to the inside of the leg, as shown in photo H. This mark should form a 90° angle with the top of the leg.

3. Using two clamps, clamp the leg in place on your worksurface. Cut the angle with a circular saw, as shown in photo I. Repeat steps 1–3 for the remaining legs. Save the off-cuts to use when clamping later (see "Attach the Legs to the Subtop," step 4 on p. 23).

5. To cut larger sheets, place the plywood on a few scrap 2x4s set flat on the floor, so the plywood won't sag as you cut. Again, make sure that the blade only protrudes under the material being cut by about ⅛". Otherwise, you risk cutting into the floor.

Even when you follow all the rules, kickbacks do occasionally occur. Just make sure that you keep both hands on the saw, and be prepared. If you are ready for a kickback, you can usually control it.

Cut with a circular saw **To cut the angle where the leg meets the subtop, clamp the board in place and use a circular saw.**

Assemble the Top

It's best to simply screw the top to the subtop instead of gluing it. Sawhorses get hard work, and if the tops are only screwed in place, they can be easily replaced with new or wider stock. Just make sure you countersink the screws and keep their placement in mind every time you cut so that you don't accidentally run a sawblade into them.

1. Cut the top and subtop to length with a circular saw. For this project, we cut them to 31", but the measurement is not critical here, so adjust it according to your needs.

2. Find the centers of both the top and the subtop—across the thickness on the subtop and across the width on the top—as shown in photo J. The most accurate way to find the center is to mark the lumber from each side. Take an educated guess at what the center measurement is (for example, across a roughly 3½"-wide 2x4, your center will be roughly 1¾"). Then mark the board by measuring and marking it the amount you guessed from each side. Split the difference

between the two marks to get the exact center. After marking the center on both the top and subtop, align the two centerlines, then clamp them in place.

3. Predrill and countersink the screws, so they won't sit proud of the top and interfere with work on the sawhorse. Countersink them about ½" so they're less likely to catch a misdirected sawblade. For more on this process, see "Drill and Countersink in One Step" on the facing page. Then screw the top and subtop together with 2" drywall screws, as shown in photo K.

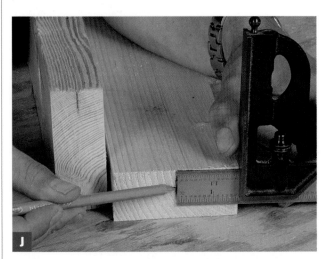

Mark out the centers Use a combination square to find the center of the top and the subtop.

Screw the top to the subtop Be sure to drive the screws well below the surface, lessening the chance that they'll hit and damage a blade.

Attach the Legs to the Subtop

1. With the top assembled, use a combination square to mark out the location for the legs. Attach them about 2" in from the ends of the subtop.

2. Predrill and countersink the screw holes in the legs and the subtop with a countersink bit and long, 3" screws, as shown in photo L.

3. Set the first leg in place, making sure it's butted squarely against the top. It helps if you rest the leg on a 2x4 to help hold it at the correct angle. Then clamp it in place. Drive in the screws, then attach the other leg on the same side of the sawhorse.

4. Once the legs on one side of the horse are secured, stand the assembly upright and slide the last two legs in place, as shown in photo M. Using the offcuts you saved when cutting the legs to fit the subtop, clamp the legs in place. Predrill and drive the screws as you did on the other leg assembly.

Attach the last leg When you attach the last two legs, clamp them in place using the offcuts you removed from the legs when you cut the angle to accept the top.

DRILL AND COUNTERSINK IN ONE STEP

Drill/drivers are handy tools to have around the shop. You'd be surprised how many screws you drive over the course of a day in the shop, and this little tool cuts your time by more than half. It allows you to predrill and countersink screws at the same time. When you're ready to drive screws, simply remove the bit, flip it end to end, and lock the driver bit in place.

It's best to buy bits in a set, which comes with a few driver bits for screws of varying sizes, as well as a few different drill bits to match the diameter of differing threads. You can change out the drivers and drill bits by loosening an Allen-head screw in the side of the barrel on the drill/driver.

Attach the first leg Because you're screwing through the narrow side of the 2x4, predrilling allows you to drive the screws without splitting the wood. Countersinking lets you get plenty of thread into the subtop using 3" screws.

Rip plywood to width Clamp a cutting guide in place and rip enough stock to make braces for both ends of the sawhorse.

Mark out the brace Use the same bevel angle you used to cut the legs, then simply extend the line with a straightedge.

Cut the angled brace Clamp the plywood in place and keep both hands on the saw. Because this isn't a critical cut, there's no reason to use a cutting guide.

Screw the end braces in place Once the end braces are cut, simply sink four screws in each to attach it to the legs.

Cut and Install End Braces

The end braces are nothing more than 9"-wide pieces of plywood cut to 15° on both sides. Not only do the braces keep the legs from wobbling, but they also butt directly against the subtop to act as a support.

1. Cut the stock to width with a circular saw and cutting guide, as shown in photo N.

2. On one end of each brace, mark a 15° angle. Use the bevel gauge to mark the angle (it should still be set to 15° from when you marked the legs). Use a straightedge to extend the line across the board, as shown in photo O. Measure and mark the width of each brace, and then mark another 15° angle with your bevel gauge at that mark.

3. Clamp the end brace to your worksurface. Use a circular saw to make the angled cuts, as shown in photo P.

4. Set each brace so it is centered on the legs and abuts the subtop, then sink drywall screws at the four corners, as shown in photo Q.

Add 2x4 Stretchers

The stretchers under this horse serve two purposes: They keep the bench from wobbling, and they are a good spot for attaching a shelf. Adding the stretchers is easy.

1. To locate the stretcher, measure down from the top and make a mark at the correct location. Hold the two 2x4s for the stretchers up to the sawhorse and mark them for length. It's best to mark their length at the top of the sawhorse rather than the bottom, just in case the legs are slightly splayed. If they are splayed, installing the stretchers will pull them into place. Then cut the stretchers to length using a circular saw.

2. Test-fit the stretchers and make sure to place them on the marks you made in step 1.

3. Screw the stretchers in place with 2½" drywall screws, as shown in photo R. Because you're drilling into end grain, it's a

Drive screws at an angle For better holding strength in end grain, drive screws in at a slight angle—about 15°.

good idea to drive your screws in at an angle—the threads of the screws will bite into the wood better. Predrill the holes to prevent them from splitting. If you're working alone, use a clamp to help you hold the stretcher in place as you're driving screws. Once the stretchers are in place, you can add the shelf.

Install a Shelf

Adding a shelf to this sawhorse isn't necessary, but it does help to stabilize the assembly. It also provides a handy place to store tools and turns your sawhorse into a good stepladder.

1. Hold the plywood for the shelf in place against the sawhorse and mark it to fit.

2. Use a circular saw to cut the plywood to size. Test-fit the shelf, as shown in

If you want to build a sawhorse that is light or easily stored, try one of these options.

Folding Sawhorse

The nice thing about this design is that it folds up for easy storage when not in use. Sides are built from either hard-wood or plywood, and the top is hinged together. Drive a bolt into one leg and use washers and screws to attach a folding latch on the other leg. Rout a groove in the latch, making sure it locks in place around the bolt head.

Knockdown Sawhorses

This design is the epitome of simplicity, and it can be easily disassembled for storage purposes. Three pieces of ply-wood are notched to fit together. A router outfitted with a straight bit is the easiest way to cut the notches—just make sure the bit matches the plywood width exactly. Though it's a knockdown design, the outward splay of the legs makes the assembled sawhorse more stable than you'd think.

Folding Sawhorse

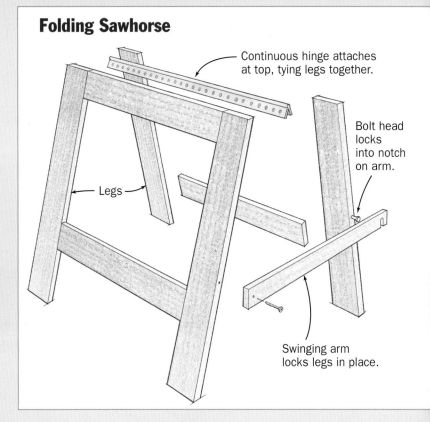

Continuous hinge attaches at top, tying legs together.

Bolt head locks into notch on arm.

Legs

Swinging arm locks legs in place.

Knockdown Sawhorse

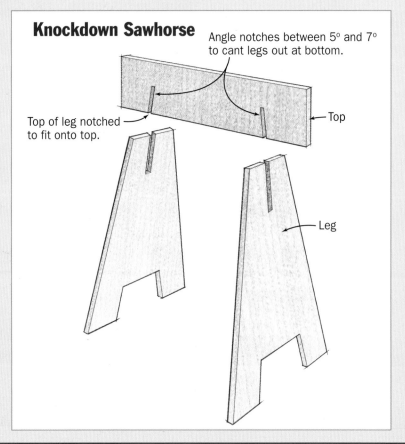

Angle notches between 5° and 7° to cant legs out at bottom.

Top of leg notched to fit onto top.

Top

Leg

Trestle Sawhorses

Many furniture makers prefer a trestle design for sawhorses because they're light, easily stored, and very sturdy. Wide feet are the key to making this a stable design. Legs are set upright, perpendicular to the floor, and notched at the top to accept a 2x6 set upright on edge. The mortises in the legs accept the stretcher and can either be cut from solid stock or formed by gluing up the legs. Dowels hold the stretcher and top in place. If you need to replace the top, simply drill out the dowels and start anew.

S

Set the shelf atop the stretchers To provide the best support to the sawhorse, size plywood for a tight fit between the legs.

photo S above. A snug fit will make for a more stable sawhorse.

3. Install the shelf in place over the stretchers with 1½" drywall screws at each corner, as shown in photo T.

4. If you'll be storing small items on the shelf, tack a ledge in place around the shelf edge to keep them from falling off. Narrow strips of scrap wood or lengths of ¼" plywood work well as a ledge.

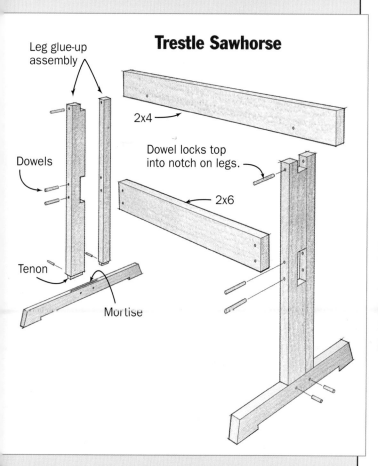

Trestle Sawhorse

Leg glue-up assembly

2x4

Dowel locks top into notch on legs.

Dowels

2x6

Tenon

Mortise

T

Attach the shelf Drywall screws at the four corners secure the shelf in place.

Workbench

The workbench is the first place you go when you need to secure work for handplaning, shaping, sanding, or assembling projects. You'll use it for everything from marking out rough stock to rubbing out the final finish with a coat of wax. It's worth your time to make sure you have a bench that can take a good beating while remaining dead flat and solidly in place.

This workbench is a very basic design, but it sacrifices nothing in the way of heft, usability, or reliability. Instead of building a trestle base from hardwoods or assembling a large cabinet-style base, you can build this table-style base using off-the-shelf lumber from your local lumberyard or home center. You may decide to add drawers later (see the Storage chapter, pp. 122–135); meanwhile, the shelf below offers a handy place to store tools.

Gluing up a benchtop can be challenging, especially with limited tooling, so this project uses a premade benchtop that can be mail-ordered and delivered to your shop two days later. Once you figure in the costs of time and materials, making your own top offers little advantage. And a premade top provides all the perks of a shopmade top. The top shown here is a 2¼"-thick maple top, but anything over 1½" will offer plenty of stability.

The heavy metal front vise allows you to clamp work on edge along the face of the bench. If you drill dog holes in the top, you'll be able to clamp work flat to the benchtop across the width of the bench.

What You'll Learn

- **Constructing strong butt joints**
- **Using a biscuit joiner**
- **Using a drilling guide**
- **Installing through and lag bolts**
- **Using a plunge router**
- **Cutting a large mortise**

Drilling guide for straight holes Until you're ready to buy a drill press for your shop, a drilling guide can help you align a portable drill to bore straight.

Some woodworkers spend—literally—years building their bench. This project proves that a quality bench that will serve you for years can be built in a weekend. If you want to add bells and whistles sometime in the future, you can. This basic design is very adaptable, so feel free to add or modify it to best suit your needs. You can add storage drawers (see the Storage chapter, pp. 122–135), you can add another vise, or you can substitute your own benchtop made from several sheets of plywood.

The base of a workbench needs to be sturdy to resist wracking under use. This base is held together with double rows of biscuits reinforced with bolts. Biscuits are a quick means to join two pieces of wood and can be used to make bookcases, cabinets, and a host of other useful furniture for your home or workshop.

It might seem simple to install bolts, but alignment is critical when drilling bolt holes, and there is some finesse involved. If you have a drill press to ensure that the holes are straight and square, it's easier work. Here, we use an inexpensive drilling guide to accomplish the same task.

In this project, we use a plunge router to cut the large mortise for the vise. Mortises are used in woodworking for many purposes, including joinery and hardware installation. In this mortise, the only critical part is the depth, but using a plunge router makes it easy work.

Biscuits help align joints Biscuits add strength, but they also make large, awkward assemblies easier to manage—even before glue is added.

A Smart Workbench

Built using a premade benchtop, metal vise, and lumber easily found at any hardware store, this workbench features a wide, flat worksurface and plenty of heft to keep it from shifting as you work.

Benchtop

Hardwood skirt

Mortise fits over face of vise

2x4 stretcher

Front vise

Lag screws and washers secure base to top.

Two biscuits secure upper stretchers.

#20 biscuits

Four biscuits secure lower stretchers.

4x4 leg

Plywood shelf

2x6 stretcher

Notches in plywood shelf fit around legs.

Brass nut accepts bench bolt.

Bench bolt and washer

Drilled hole accepts nut for bench bolt.

Lag screw and washer

FRONT

2 1/4"
3/4"
61 1/2"
60"
3/4"
1"
13 3/4"
8 1/4"
Skirt
39 1/2"
32 1/2"
33 1/2"
3/4"
35 3/4"
5 1/2"
3 1/2"
5 1/2"
6"
3 1/2"

SIDE

24 3/4"
24"
Benchtop
2"
2 3/4"
20"
2x4 stretcher
13"
4x4 leg
2x6 stretcher
3 1/2"
3 1/2"
3 1/2"

Quantity	Part	Actual Size	What to Buy
8	Lag screws	⅜" x 5"	
4	Lag screws	⅜" x 4½"	
11	Lag screws	¼" x 2"	
8	Bench bolts	½" x 6"	Cross dowel type with barrel nut
1 box	Screws	#6 x 2"	Wood screws
24	Biscuits	#20	A container full. You'll need some for practice.
1	Bench vise	¾" x 10" x 4"	Buy the largest you can afford. If necessary, adjust the size to fit your vise. Quick-release is preferable.
1	Benchtop	24" x 60"	1½"- to 2½"-thick laminated hard maple
1	Front skirt	¾" x 5½" x 61½"	1" x 6" x 10' hard maple will yield the three skirt parts.
2	Side skirt	¾" x 5½" x 24½"	
4	Legs	3½" x 3½" x 33¼"	Two 6' pine or fir 4x4s
2	Lower long stretchers, front and back	1½" x 5½" x 32½"	One 10' pine or fir 2x6 yields lumber for all lower stretchers.
2	Lower side stretchers	1½" x 5½" x 13"	
2	Upper long stretchers, front and back	1½" x 3½" x 32½"	One 10' pine or fir 2x4 yields lumber for all upper stretchers.
2	Upper side stretchers	1½" x 3½" x 13½"	
1	Shelf	¾" x 18" x 37½"	2' x 4' (¼ sheet) birch plywood will yield bottom shelf and end stop (see pp. 52–54).
1	Filler block	Size to vise	Scraps of maple from skirt
3	Spacers	¾" thick	Scraps of plywood
1 box	Drywall screws	1½"	
	Misc.		Yellow glue, sandpaper, finish

Buying Materials

All the stock for the base can be found at any home center or hardware store. The four legs are cut to length from 4x4s, and the stretchers are all cut from 2x4s and 2x6s. Note that the nominal size of framing lumber (2x4) differs from actual size (1½" x 3½"). Similarly, hardwoods sold in home centers as 1x are actually ¾" in thickness. Whenever you choose lumber, remember to check for bow, warp, and twist as well as cracks or loose knots.

The benchtop can be ordered from woodworking retailers (see Sources, p. 166), or you can buy a section of butcher-block countertop from a home center. You'll be able to buy most of the hardware from a hardware store or home center, but the bench bolts must be ordered from Lee Valley Tools (see Sources, p. 166). Bolts and square nuts can be substituted but will require cutting a mortise with a plunge router to access the nut.

TOOLS

- Combination square
- Tape measure
- Awl
- Biscuit joiner
- Plunge router
- Circular saw
- Miter saw (optional)
- Jigsaw or handsaw (optional)
- 1" chisel
- Mallet
- Cordless drill
- 1⅛" Forstner bit
- ¾" Forstner bit
- ⅜" drill bit
- ⅜" brad-point drill bit
- ½" drill bit
- ½" brad-point drill bit
- ¾" spade bit
- ¼" brad-point drill bit
- #4 or #5 handplane
- Block plane
- Drilling guide or drill press
- Two 4'-long clamps
- Socket wrench kit
- Masking tape
- Pencil

The Workbench

Before you cut any lumber, purchase your vise, hardware, and benchtop. Exact dimensions will depend on these items, and it's easier to make adjustments to your plan with your materials on hand.

Building the Base

The base of this bench is a table-style base—it's got four legs, an apron at the top, and stretchers around the bottom. Once you've built this bench, you will understand the basic joinery that goes into making a table and should be able to build a table of any size.

This base is sized to accommodate a large (10" wide) quick-release front vise on the left side of the bench. If your vise will allow you to build a longer base, it will add more stability.

Workbench Base

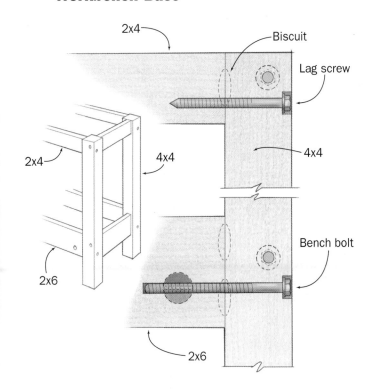

Find the right height To find the workbench height that's right for you, stand with your hand down and your palm to the floor. The distance between the floor and your palm is your ideal bench height.

The height of the base is just right for someone about 5'10"; if you're a little taller or shorter, adjust accordingly. Benches range from anywhere between 30" and 40" tall—it depends somewhat on your height and the length of your arms. In my experience, the most efficient bench height is somewhere between your waist and your hip—it should be about the height of the heel of your hand when you stand upright and have your hands by your sides, as shown in photo A. For a user who is 5' 9", a height between 35" and 36" is usually about right.

Cut the legs and stretchers to length

Untreated 4x4 posts make up the legs on this bench, but two 2x4s glued or screwed together could serve the same purpose. The stretchers are nothing more than 2x4s around the top and 2x6s near the bottom. If you want a clean look, you can run them through a planer before you start cutting, but it's really not necessary. Both the legs and the stretchers can be cut to length using a miter saw. If you're without a miter saw, a circular saw will do the same job.

B

Cut legs to length **Be sure to clamp your work in place and see that the offcut is supported.**

C

Chamfer the hard edges **To soften those bumps against the bench, ease the corners—of the legs and all other exposed edges—by knocking off the hard edge with a block plane.**

To cut the legs with a circular saw, in order to reach full depth, you'll have to cut one side, then flip the piece over and cut the opposite face.

1. For reference, establish one square end on each leg by measuring slightly longer than the length of one leg and crosscutting it with the miter saw, as shown in photo B. Mark each freshly cut end to help you remember which ones are square.

2. Measure the leg length you determined for your bench with a tape measure hooked on a square end. Mark all four legs to the same length. Just to be sure, you can lay out the legs next to one another on the floor and align the square ends. Your marks should all line up.

3. Line up the blade to your mark, just on the waste side of the line, and crosscut each leg to length. Double-check to make sure all legs are the same length.

If you're using 4x4s, the legs will already be rounded over by the mill. If you're using freshly milled lumber, you may want to soften the hard edges of the legs—and the stretchers, too—by chamfering the edges with a block plane, as shown in photo C.

After preparing the legs, the next step is to mark off and cut the biscuit slots. If you've never used a biscuit joiner before, a few practice cuts would be a good idea.

What You'll Need

- **Biscuit joiner**
- **#20 biscuits**
- **¾"-thick scrap lumber at least 5" wide**

The biscuit joiner (sometimes referred to as a plate joiner) is a simple tool that does one thing really well: cut mating arched slots that accept football-shaped biscuits. To join two pieces, simply cut biscuit slots in both pieces, insert glue and a biscuit into one slot, then slide the mating piece in place and clamp it up until the glue dries. The biscuit is made of compressed wood. Once glue penetrates the wood, the biscuit swells up, locking the joint tight.

The fence, which can be set at a variety of angles, is a reference surface from which the distance to the slot is set. The slot is usually cut in the center of the board for one biscuit or stacked one about ½" above the other for double biscuits. If you want to use even more biscuits, add rows of double biscuits side by side, with at least ½" between them.

1. Make several pencil marks on the edge of the board approximately 2" from each end and 4" from one another. Set the fence to cut at 90° and tighten the lock knob. Move the height adjuster to cut a slot in the center of the board.

2. Clamp the board firmly to your work-surface. Make sure the clamp position won't interfere with your cut. Align the center mark of the biscuit joiner with your pencil mark.

3. Press the on switch, allow the biscuit joiner to reach full speed, and plunge forward into the workpiece. Let the blade retract completely before moving the machine. When you

remove the biscuit joiner, you'll find a slot that accepts a biscuit.

Unfortunately, sometimes the fence is out of square or moves slightly between the time you cut one slot and then cut its mate. Or you wobble slightly, and the cut is not exactly at 90°. But the solution is simple: rely on the base of the biscuit joiner rather than the fence. If you need to offset a joint—when you're "supposed" to use the fence—use spacers to do so. Try making the same cuts on the opposite face of the board with the fence retracted and a flat surface as your "fence."

Since this method is more reliable, we'll use it for this project. But there are times when you'll want to use the fence, especially for 45° biscuit slots, so it's worth learning how to make accurate cuts with it.

Biscuit the legs and stretchers

The stretchers and legs on this bench are joined with double rows of #20 biscuits. Because the joints are reinforced with bench bolts or lag screws, you could get by with a single row of biscuits to keep the stretchers aligned. But cutting two rows takes only seconds more and provides a much stronger joint. Some would argue that adding lag screws and bench bolts is overkill, but because a bench gets the hardest of work, I like the insurance.

For accuracy, we're using spacers to register where the biscuit joiner will cut the slot. Use scraps of ¾" plywood as spacers.

1. Start biscuiting on two adjacent faces. Mark out centerlines according to the drawing below and then place the legs on the benchtop or another reliably flat surface. Make sure the legs are placed so that the outer face is facing up and the fence on your biscuit joiner is removed or out of the way.

2. To cut the outer row of biscuits, use three spacers and align the centering mark on the biscuit joiner and the centerline on the leg, as shown in photo D. On the bottom of the leg, you'll cut two biscuit slots with the spacers in place. Then remove one of the spacers, align the cut, and cut another two biscuits, as shown in photo E. Then move to the top of the leg, put all three spacers back in place, and cut one biscuit. Then remove one spacer and cut one biscuit. Repeat the same process on the adjacent face of the leg and then the other three legs.

Leg Diagram

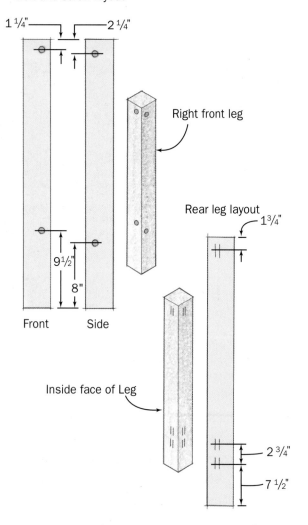

Bolt and screw layout

1 ¼"   2 ¼"

Right front leg

9 ½"

8"

Front   Side

Rear leg layout

1 ¾"

Inside face of Leg

2 ¾"

7 ½"

WORK SMART

Until you're ready attach the new benchtop, set it on two sawhorses to make an instant workbench. Just make sure to protect the top from damage by using scrap under pieces you'll be drilling through.

Biscuit the legs To cut the outer row of biscuits on the legs, use three spacers to cut the outer row of slots on the legs. Make sure the outside face of the leg is facing up before you cut.

Cut the inner biscuit slots To cut the inner row of biscuit slots on the legs, simply remove one of the spacers and repeat the cuts.

Biscuit the stretchers Mark centerlines for the biscuit cuts, and use a piece of ¾" plywood as a spacer to cut the inner row of biscuits.

Cut the second row of biscuits After removing the spacer block, cut the outer row of biscuits on all the stretchers.

3. To biscuit the stretchers, you'll use the same spacers, but you'll only need one. Mark out the biscuit centerlines on the ends of the stretchers, place the stretchers face up on the benchtop, and set a single spacer in place to make the first cuts, as shown in photo F. Then remove the spacer and make the bottom row of cuts, as shown in photo G. Repeat the

process on the ends of all the stretchers. The biscuiting process moves very quickly—all the plunge cuts take only about 15 minutes.

Test all of the slots with a dry biscuit to make sure that you've cut to full depth. You may also want to dry-fit adjacent parts to check alignment.

Countersink and drill holes in the legs

To make sure the base of this bench is rock solid, use lag screws and bench bolts to reinforce the joints. I chose ⅜" x 5" lag screws for the sides and large ½" x 6" bench bolts to secure the long stretchers. Countersink and predrill screw and bolt holes before the bench goes together to ease installation.

Drilling accurate, square holes for the screws and bolts is critical for assembly. Use a drilling guide set to 90° to ensure that the holes are drilled true. If you have a drill press, it makes the job even easier.

1. Locate the centerpoints of the holes according to the drawing (see the drawing on p. 36), then use a drill guide outfitted with a 1⅛" Forstner bit to drill the counter-sink, as shown in photo H. To bury the heads of the bolts and screws, aim for a ½"-deep countersink.

BENCH BOLTS

Bench bolts are a great invention. They're big, strong bolts with hex heads, and they screw into large brass nuts. To join the legs to the long stretchers, the bolt goes through the leg, and the brass nut is set into a hole drilled into the stretcher. They offer plenty of strength to keep the bench joints tight. If you think you'll ever want to take your bench apart, don't add glue. Otherwise, the glue only adds to the strength of the joint. If the bench ever wiggles its way loose, just tighten up the bench bolts until the base is nice and solid again.

2. Once the countersink is drilled, use the centerpoint created by the Forstner bit to locate the bit to predrill for the lag screws, as shown in photo I. Use a piece of scrap under your workpiece to avoid drilling into your worksurface. Use a ⅜" brad-point bit in the drilling guide. Predrill for the short end stretchers.

3. Use a ½" brad-point bit to predrill for the large bench bolts that connect the ends to the long stretchers.

H

Countersink for lag screw Use a 1⅛" Forstner bit and a drilling guide to drill countersink holes in the outside faces of the legs.

I

Predrill for lag screw Drill holes to accept the lag screws and bench bolts that secure the legs to the stretchers. Use a piece of scrap under your workpiece to prevent tearout.

Drill holes for bench bolts in the stretchers

1. Before assembling anything, drill the holes in the long stretchers that accept the nuts for the bench bolts. Locate the centerpoint according to the drawing on p. 36 and drill all the way through the stretcher with a 1⅛" Forstner bit and drill guide, as shown in photo J. If you want a clean look on the outside of the bench, you can stop the cut just shy of full depth, but assembly is a lot easier if you drill all the way through. It's also possible to set the nut in a 1" hole (which the directions recommend), but this leaves little room for error. If you cut your hole slightly larger, there's a little more wiggle room for connecting the bolt to the nut.

K

Assemble the front and back **Before adding any glue, set the biscuits in place and assemble all the parts one side at a time.**

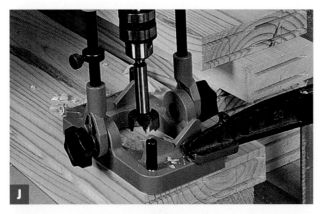

J

Drill access holes through the stretchers **Use a 1⅛" access hole through the long stretchers to accept the nut of the bench bolt.**

2. Once all the holes are drilled, dry-fit and clamp all the parts to make sure everything lines up, as shown in photo K. Leave the assembly clamped up while you drill into the stretchers.

3. You'll want to predrill the stretchers for the bench bolts to prevent splitting when you install the bolts. Use a long, ½" drill bit to drill into the long stretchers, as shown in photo L. At this point, the bit will follow the

L

Drill for bench bolts **Clamp up the front and back assembly. When the clamps are in place, use a long, ½" brad-point bit to predrill into the stretchers.**

hole you've already put in the leg, so there's no need to use a drilling guide. You can wait to predrill the short stretchers for lag screws until gluing and assembly is complete.

Assembling the Base

Assembly is a tense time in any woodworking project. Once the glue is applied, time is short to get everything correctly in place and the clamps tight. That's why dry-fitting is so important. Identify and correct any problems in alignment or assembly based on the dry-fit you did in step 2 on p. 39. Come up with a strategy for which parts to put together first and for organizing and positioning your clamps to have them handy when you need them.

Assemble the ends

1. At this point, you're ready to assemble the ends. Set out your clamps as you did during dry-fitting. It also helps to have a no-mar mallet nearby, just in case you need to tap parts into place for a tight fit. Start by gluing up the short ends. Lay a thin layer of glue on all the biscuit slots and surrounding joint areas. Dab a little glue on the biscuits and put the biscuits in the slots, as shown in photo A. Press all the parts together.

2. Clamp up the ends flat on the benchtop. When you position the clamps, make sure you locate them so they're clear of the countersink holes.

3. Once the clamps are in place, measure the diagonals to check the assembly for square. If necessary, adjust the clamps until the two diagonal measurements are exactly the same, as shown in photo B.

4. Once the assembly is square, use a ⅜" drill bit to predrill for the lag screws. The holes you drilled in the legs will serve to guide the bit to cut square and true. Use masking tape to mark the length of the lag screw on the bit. When you drill to the depth of the tape, you'll know the hole is the proper depth, as shown in photo C. Drill the holes for all lag screws in the ends.

5. Hand-tighten the lag screws with a socket wrench. Because you're screwing into a soft wood that could strip out, don't overtighten the lag screws; all you need is the washer to bottom out and to feel a little resistance on the wrench, as shown in photo D.

A

Add glue When gluing up with biscuits, make sure you get a thin layer of glue on the biscuits, as well as in and around the biscuit slots. The keyword is *thin*—using a thick layer of glue won't make the joint any stronger, but it'll make cleanup harder.

Check for square The easiest way to check squareness is to measure the two diagonals from corner to corner. If they're not exactly the same, use clamps to pull the assembly square.

Drill stretchers to accept the lag screws Use a long, ⅜" bit to drill the stretchers to accept the lag screws. Follow the path of the holes already drilled through the legs, then use a piece of tape to mark the correct depth.

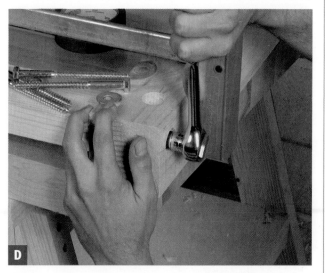

Tighten up the lag screws Once the assembly is square, set the lag screws in place and tighten them down with a socket wrench. Be sure to use a washer to keep from crushing the wood on the legs.

Connect the ends

Once the ends have dried—an hour is plenty of time—repeat the same process to join the ends together with the long stretchers.

1. Set one end flat on the floor and lay on the glue, again in the biscuit slots of both the legs and the long stretchers. Dab some glue on the biscuits and place them in the slots of the legs.

E

Assemble the base Once the ends are assembled, set the biscuits in place, add glue, and then install the long stretchers.

2. Connect the long stretchers to the end on the floor and quickly lay the glue onto the biscuit slots of the opposite stretcher ends and the other end assembly. Insert the biscuits and position the end, aligning the biscuits, then press it onto the rest of the assembly, as shown in photo E.

3. Now, you can pick up the assembly—taking care to hold it together—and put on some 4' clamps. The clamps are really just an extra hand to hold the assembly together until you can get the bench bolts in place and tightened up. Once they're installed, the clamps can be removed.

F

Install bench bolt Push the bolt into place and shift the brass nut until the bolt threads line up. A socket wrench pulls everything together. Tighten down enough so that the nut embeds itself in the soft wood of the stretcher.

4. Install the brass nut of the bench bolt into the hole you drilled in the stretcher with the slot side facing out, as shown in photo F. The hole in the nut must be lined up with the hole you cut in the leg and the stretcher. If not, you can use a screwdriver to rotate the nut until it lines up correctly.

5. With the washer near the bolt head, push the bench bolt through until it contacts the nut. Then tighten the bolt with a socket wrench. It helps to put some pressure on the brass nut to hold it in place until the screw begins to grab the threads in the nut.

6. Once the bolts are tightened, you can remove the clamps. Clean any glue that has squeezed out with a sharp chisel.

G

Remove the squeeze-out When glue is beginning to harden—about 30 minutes after it goes on—you can easily cut away the squeeze-out with a chisel.

Install a Shelf

Adding a shelf to this bench provides a good spot for storing tools. And when it comes to workbenches, the heavier they are, the better. There's really no need to over-think the shelf—it's just a piece of ¾" plywood cut to size, with cutouts in the corners to fit around the legs. A jigsaw or handsaw makes the cut easily, but you'll get slightly better results with a circular saw.

1. Measure across the lower stretchers to find the exact width and length of the plywood you'll need for the shelf. It will look better and catch less dust if the edges of the ply-wood are flush to the outside faces of the stretchers. Measure and mark the plywood.

2. To cut the plywood to size, use your circular saw. Start by measuring out the offset from the edge of the base on your circular saw to the blade, then measure out that distance from the marked line along the length of the cut. Using a cutting guide ensures a straight cut (see "A Shopmade Cutting Guide" on p. 19). Cut the sheet to length and width, as shown in photo A.

3. To measure for the cutouts, get the width directly off the bench by holding the shelf against the legs, as shown in photo B.

4. Saw as accurately as possible when making the cutouts for the legs to prevent having to adjust the cuts later. If you use a circular saw, there will be a small piece of wood left uncut on the underside of the shelf—just finish off the cut with a handsaw.

5. Put the shelf in place and drive drywall screws through the plywood into the stretchers to attach it, as shown in photo C.

Trim the corners With the shelf clamped in place and cut to size, use a circular saw to trim the corners to fit around the leg.

Rip the shelf to width To cut the plywood to width, set it atop two sawhorses and use a long cutting guide to ensure a straight cut with a circular saw.

Screw down the shelf Once the shelf is in place, a few drywall screws secure it to the stretchers.

The Benchtop

For the bench built here, a premade bench-top is used. Manufactured tops are available by mail-order from woodworking catalogs, or you can buy a length of butcher-block countertop from your local home center or cabinet shop—just make sure you're getting a real wood butcher block and not a faux-wood countertop. Most commercial tops are made from hard maple, and it's the best choice.

In the end, the price of a purchased benchtop is about the same as that of buying the hardwood yourself and doing all the work of cutting the stock, gluing it together, and then flattening the top. A benchtop needs to be dead-on flat, so unless you are really confident about your handplane skills, it's best to avoid making your own solid wood top.

If you're set on making your own bench-top, you can also glue up three layers of plywood or MDF and then edge it with hardwood. It's a good solution if you want to save some money and don't mind replacing the top at some point, since it won't have the life span of a thick hardwood benchtop.

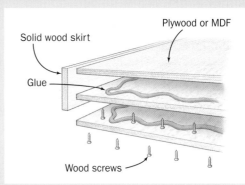
The easiest way to build a thick, flat bench-top is to glue and screw together three pieces of plywood (or MDF) and install a hardwood skirt around the edge. So the screws aren't seen on the benchtop, screw through the middle section into the top, and then add the lower section and screw through it into the middle section. Be sure to locate screws so that they won't interfere with the vises or bench dogs you're planning to use.

For laying the glue onto the faces of the plywood, try using a 4" roller designed for painting trim. And if you use MDF for the top surface, a couple of penetrating coats of Watco® or shellac will help preserve it.

Benchtop

The overhang on the left provides clearance for the vise. If you're right-handed, locate the face vise on the left. If you're a lefty, reverse the location of the vise.

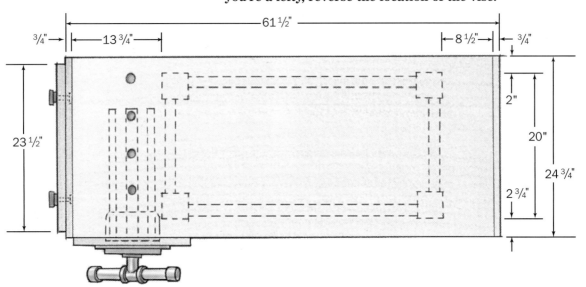

Installing a Vise

The vise on this bench is a quick-release version with metal jaws. The quick-release mechanism is handy, as it allows you to lift up on the vise handle and pull out the front face to whatever depth you choose. It's a lot better than cranking the vise to the correct depth every time you need to adjust it. It also has a built-in bench dog that pulls up from the front jaw. When used in conjunction with bench dogs on the benchtop, the vise's dog helps you secure work flat to the top of the bench.

The vise used on this bench is one of the largest you can buy—it's 10" wide and allows a 12" opening—but a smaller one will do most of the same work. If you shop around, you can find quick-release vises for as little as $30, but before you skimp on a vise, be sure the action is smooth and that it offers at least a 7" opening—even after the skirt and face have been installed.

A

Position the vise and mark pilot holes With the filler block screwed in place, use the vise template to mark holes with an awl. If the template is missing, use the vise itself to mark the holes.

Securing the Vise to the Bench

A metal vise attaches to your benchtop using lag screws, but make sure the top of the vise sits below the benchtop.

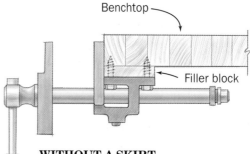

Benchtop

Filler block

WITHOUT A SKIRT
To attach a vise to a benchtop with no skirt, add a filler block thick enough to bring the top of the vise at least ½" below the top of the bench.

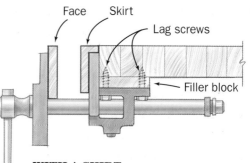

Face Skirt

Lag screws

Filler block

WITH A SKIRT
If your bench has a skirt, add the vise first. The skirt is mortised around the face of the vise, and a wooden face is attached to the front jaw of the vise.

B

Rout to the correct depth Set the depth of the bit to the thickness of the vise and rout out the waste between the drilled holes. It's best to stay away from the edges of the mortises—they're best removed with a chisel and mallet.

Secure the vise to the bench

Vises can be mounted to the front of the benchtop in at least two ways: You can screw the vise to the bench, then cut a mortise in a skirt to fit over the face, or you can mortise the benchtop to allow the vise to sit flush to the front edge of the top. I find it easier to attach the vise to the benchtop, then mortise a skirt to fit over the vise. If you go this route, you leave yourself more options for changing out vises in the future.

The vise should sit about ½" to ¾" below the benchtop, which means you'll probably need to install a filler block to the bottom of the bench (see the drawings on p. 45 and at right).

1. To determine the filler block's thickness, flip over the top surface of the bench so that it is facing down, position the vise, and set a scrap of plywood in place to act as a filler block. Try different thicknesses of stock until the distance from the top of the vise jaw to the top of the benchtop is at least ½".

Secure the vise Butt the vise tight to the edge of the bench and drive lag screws through the filler block and into the benchtop.

Protect Your Work

The jaws of a metal vise will scar your work if it is not covered. It's a good idea to mortise a wooden skirt around the vise and add a wooden face to the front jaw of the vise.

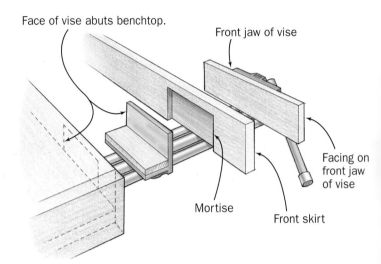

Face of vise abuts benchtop.

Front jaw of vise

Facing on front jaw of vise

Mortise

Front skirt

2. Drill pilot holes, countersink, and then screw the filler block to the underside of the benchtop (now facing up). Make sure your screws won't interfere with the screws in the bottom of the vise.

3. Once the filler block is screwed to the benchtop, use the template provided with the vise to locate screw holes on the bottom and front of the vise. This way, you can attach the vise directly to the filler block and the front of the bench, as shown in photo A.

4. With the holes marked, drill pilot holes for the mounting screws. Most vises provide lag screws to secure the vise to the bottom of the bench—just make sure they're long enough to sink into the benchtop about 1". The front of the vise is mounted with plain wood screws that sit in countersunk holes machined into the vise, as shown in photo B.

Mortise the front skirt

Because the router base needs a solid surface to rest on when you're cutting the mortise, use a 1x6 for the skirt. Once the mortise is cut, you can trim off the bottom portion of the skirt (see the drawing on the facing page).

1. The first step in mortising the skirt is to measure the depth, height, and width of the vise, then to transfer all those measurements to the skirt, as shown in photos D and E on p. 48.

2. With the mortise marked out on the skirt, hog off the bulk of the waste using a large Forstner bit—you can use the same 1⅛" bit you used to countersink the legs, as shown in photo F on p. 48. In most cases, the depth of the bit is less than the depth of the mortise, which makes stopping short of full depth

---

SKILL BUILDER: Routing Freehand

What You'll Need

- **Plunge router**
- **Forstner bit**
- **⅜" straight bit**
- **Clamps**
- **Hearing and eye protection**

To hog off the waste on the mortise in the front skirt, routing is a good choice. If you've never routed freehand before (without a bearing, edge guide, or fence), you should probably practice to get a feel for it.

1. Mount a ⅜" straight bit in the router and set the depth of cut by adjusting the guide rod. Some routers, like the one I'm using, allow you to set a series of progressively deeper depths. You want to avoid hogging off all the waste in one deep cut, as it might put too much pressure on the bit, causing it to break.

2. Mark off an area to rout in some scrap. Clamp it securely, but make sure the clamps won't interfere with the baseplate.

3. Drill some holes with a Forstner bit to remove some of the waste.

4. When you start the cut, plunge down into a predrilled hole and slowly work away at the islands of wood left between the drilled holes. Take shallow cuts—no more than ¼" at a time.

5. You can rout near the edges, but don't try to get too close, or the bit could dig into the wood. Check where you are by looking through the viewing window. Make sure you wear eye protection.

easy, but you can also place a piece of tape on the bit to denote the stopping point.

3. Use a plunge router outfitted with a ⅜" straight bit to remove the bulk of the waste. For more on this process, see "Skill Builder: Routing Freehand" on p. 47 and photo B on p. 45. There's no reason to remove every last bit of wood between the drilled holes. The big "islands" of wood left behind can be easily

F

Hog out the waste **Drill overlapping holes with a Forstner bit, and make sure not to go too deep. In this case, the depth of the bit was just under the depth of the mortise. Otherwise, apply tape to the bit to serve as a guide.**

D

Measure for the mortise **Mark the top of your skirt against the vise and use it as a reference point to transfer all measurements from the vise location to the skirt.**

G

Chisel the remaining waste **A soft touch with a chisel defines the edges and chips away the remaining stock.**

knocked off with a chisel once the router has established the depth of the mortise.

4. After routing, you'll still need to clean up the edges of the mortise using a wide chisel (1" or more) and mallet. To clean up the edges, place the chisel on the mortise line, then give it a few hard raps with the mallet. To knock off the islands of wood left by the router, place the chisel bevel side down in the mortise and give it a few light taps, as shown in photo G. The wood should pop off pretty easily.

E

Mark out the mortise **Once the height, width, and depth of the mortise are marked out, crosshatch the area to be removed.**

Attach the skirts

With the front skirt mortised to a good fit over the vise, simply set it in place and use 2" lag screws to secure it to the side of the benchtop, as shown in photo H.

1. Use clamps to line up the top of the skirt with the top of the bench and clamp it in place.

Add facing to the front face A well-fitted mortise will sit in place on the vise and pull tight to the front of the benchtop.

Secure the skirt Lag screws set into countersunk, predrilled holes secure the skirt tight to the benchtop and provide a solid surface for clamping work around the edge of the bench.

2. Then countersink and predrill the holes for lag screws. Use a socket wrench to drive the screws home, as shown in photo I.

3. Attach the side skirts in the same way, but if you intend to make the bench stop (see pp. 52–54), hold off on attaching the skirt on the vise side of the bench or simply plan to remove it to install the carriage bolts for the bench stop.

Add a wooden jaw

Metal vises are great inventions that save woodworkers countless hours of building their own. But to keep from denting workpieces when you tighten up the vise, you'll need to add a wooden jaw to the front of the vise.

1. Cut a length of maple (or other hardwood) to the width of the skirt and just long enough to cover the width of the front jaw.

2. Screw the wooden jaw in place using the holes in the metal jaw, as shown in photo J.

Face the front jaw A length of hardwood screwed to the front jaw of the vise keeps workpieces from being marred by the metal vise. Install the facing though predrilled holes using wood screws.

Plane the skirts flush

If the front skirt or facing on the front jaw of the vise winds up a little proud of the top, simply trim it flush with a #4 or #5 handplane. Once the jaw is in place, take light passes off the skirt and jaw with a handplane, as shown in photo K. You'll know the skirt is flush when you begin to remove the tiniest of shavings from the benchtop itself. Stop there. When you hang the side skirts on the ends, trim them flush as well.

K

Flush up the top To bring the skirt flat to the top of the benchtop, set a #4 or #5 handplane for a light cut and plane your work slowly.

> ### WORK SMART
>
> When planing two pieces flush, check the difference in height frequently with your fingertips until you can just barely feel the difference. Lighten up on your plane cuts as you get close to avoid cutting into the lower piece.

Drilling the Dog Holes

Large metal vises come with a built-in bench dog that slides up from the front face. To use this dog, drill at least one hole in line with the vise's bench dog, as shown in photo A. I prefer to drill a row of holes—about 4" or 5" apart—so that I'll be able to accommodate workpieces of varying widths and still keep the bulk of the work on the benchtop.

The good thing about using a thick maple benchtop is that maple is a hard, dense wood that won't scratch or mar easily. The downside is that when it comes time to drill holes in your bench, you'll be in for a bit of work.

A Forstner bit will make the cut without causing too much tearout, but it's slow, hard work that threatens to burn up even a heavy-duty drill, not to mention dull your bit. A

A

Put the dogs to use Drilling dog holes allows you to use bench dogs to secure work flat to the benchtop.

spade bit will make the cut rather easily, but it will also leave unsightly tearout on the top of your bench. The best option I've found is to use a combination of bits.

1. Measure off the location for your dog holes indicating with an X where the centerpoint should be.

2. Start with a ¾" Forstner bit and cut just deep enough—about ½"—to make sure that there's no tearout on the benchtop.

3. Then move to a ¼" brad-point bit, making sure to start the bit in the centerpoint left at the bottom of the hole from the Forstner bit.

4. The final hole can then be drilled all the way through the benchtop with a ¾" spade bit as shown in photo B.

B

> ## WORK SMART
>
> You can also use your drilling guide to make sure your dog holes are straight, especially for drilling the initial cuts with the Forstner bit.

Drill the dog holes Cutting through a thick maple benchtop means progressing through a series of bits: a Forstner bit, a brad point bit, and, finally, a spade bit. Use a square to help keep the bit aligned.

Attaching the Top and Choosing a Finish

Because wood expands and contracts with changes in humidity, you don't want to screw down the benchtop on the front and back edges. If you do, you're just asking for it to crack. Four lag screws—two each on the ends—are plenty to anchor the top to the base. Set the top in place and predrill ⅜" holes through the top end stretchers and into the benchtop. You'll want the holes no more than 5" apart and centered on the ends. Countersinking is not necessary here, but make sure that at least 1" of thread engages in the top.

I prefer a light oil-based finish for the top. Opt for boiled linseed oil or a varnish thinned down with about 50 percent mineral spirits. Truth be told, a nice coat of wax works just fine—wipe it on, wait 5 minutes, then wipe it off. You just want to make sure there's something on the surface so that you'll be able to clean up glue spills without sanding or scraping away the worksurface.

Bench Stop

Traditional benches have an end vise that allows you to clamp work down to the bench for handplaning or shaping. But you can get almost the same function—and with much less fuss—out of a bench stop installed on the vise end of the bench. Building and installing one takes only a very short time, a scrap of plywood, and simple hardware you'll find at most hardware stores. If you're left-handed, install the bench stop on the opposite end.

Cut a piece of ¾" plywood to the dimensions shown in the drawing on the facing page. If you've cut the shelf for the workbench carefully, you should have a piece of scrap large enough to make the stop.

1. Before installing the end skirt (or if you've already installed the skirt, just unscrew the lag screws), clamp it to a piece of plywood that will serve as a bench stop. Measure the

Work against the stop Grooves in the bench stop make quick work of adjusting it up for use or down and out of the way. To use it, set the height to just under the height of the stock you're working.

MATERIALS

Quantity	Part	Actual Size	What to Buy
2	Carriage bolts	⅜" x 2"	
2	Round washers	⅜" dia. opening	
2	T-handles		Jig handle to fit ⅜" screws
1	Bench stop	¾" x 7½" x 23½"	Use plywood left over from shelf.

Bench Stop

Traditional workbenches are outfitted with an end vise as well as a front vise, but a bench stop serves most of the same functions and is easily installed.

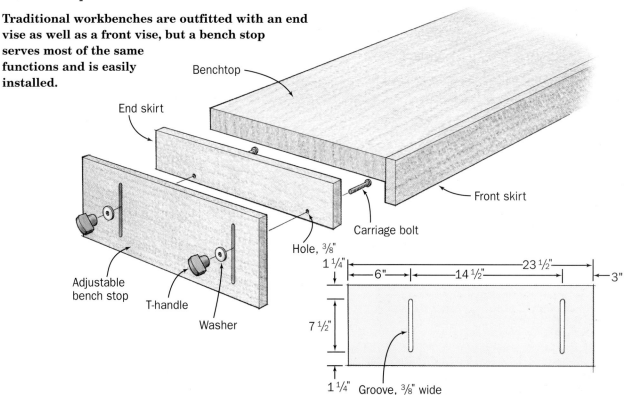

Benchtop

End skirt

Front skirt

Carriage bolt

Hole, 3/8"

Adjustable bench stop

T-handle

Washer

1 1/4"

6"

14 1/2"

23 1/2"

3"

7 1/2"

1 1/4" Groove, 3/8" wide

location for the carriage bolts and drill two 3/8" holes through both the skirt and the plywood for the stop, as shown in photo A.

2. On the bench stop, mark out lines denoting the full width of the drilled hole and draw out the slot you'll cut with the router, as shown in photo B on p. 54.

3. Using a straight piece of stock as a guide, rout through the bench stop using a 3/8" router bit mounted in a plunge router, as shown in photo C. Take light cuts, no more

than 1/4" at a time, until you get nearly to the other side. It's better to leave a wafer-thin piece at the bottom rather than cut all the way through. You can cut through the thin section with a utility knife.

A

Drill the stop and skirt Before attaching the end skirt to the left end of the vise, drill holes through both the skirt and the end stop.

WORK SMART

A bench stop works well for working wood against it, but it's also a good idea to raise it when you're working on projects that may tip and fall off the end of the bench.

B

Mark out the grooves Mark lines along the drilled hole in the end stop and mark endpoints that allow it to rest below the benchtop when not in use.

C

Rout the grooves Use the straight edge of a scrap of plywood to guide your plunge router outfitted with a ⅜" straight bit. Take several light passes— no more than ¼" deep at a time—until you've cut through to the underside.

D

Install the bench stop Carriage bolts go through the end skirt and slide onto the grooves in the bench stop. T-handles make it easy to raise and lower the stop.

4. Test to see that the slots in the bench stop line up with the holes on the end skirt and drop the carriage bolts in place, as shown in photo D.

5. If the fit is a little tight, open up the slots on the bench stop with a file. Once the two fit together easily, you can go ahead and install the end skirt.

6. Set the carriage bolts in place, set the end stop in place, and install the washers and T-handles.

7. To use the stop, simply loosen both T-handles and slide the stop into position. It's best to set the height so the top of the stop is just below the workpiece.

Bench Dogs

In a traditional workbench, bench dogs were usually made of steel and square in shape. But with a premade slab, it's pretty difficult to cut square mortises, so round bench dogs are a good solution. You can put a round bench dog anywhere you can drill a ¾" hole. If you later decide to add another vise, it's simple to add more dog holes as well.

Good-quality round bench dogs are available through woodworking catalogs, but you can easily make your own. The design shown in the drawing below is quick to make, but pretty foolproof. It uses only a ¾" dowel and a square of ¼" plywood or hardwood.

A Shopmade Bench Dog

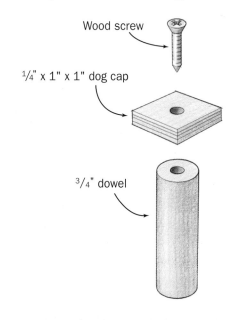

Wood screw

¼" x 1" x 1" dog cap

³/₄" dowel

PHOTO COURTESY OF LEE VALLEY TOOLS

Versatile round bench dog Soft brass dogs are outfitted with a spring-fit bar that allows them to stop at whatever depth you choose.

1. Cut ¼"-thick plywood or hardwood to 1" in width to make the caps of the dogs.

2. Cut off 1" square caps for all the bench dogs you intend to make.

3. Decide on the length of your bench dog stems. You'll want them to be about as long as the thickness of the benchtop. Then cut the dowels to length.

4. Mark the diagonals from corner to corner to find the centerpoint of each cap. Drill a pilot hole through the cap.

5. Drill a pilot hole in the center of each dowel and attach a cap to a dowel with a wood screw.

MATERIALS

Quantity	Part	Actual Size	What to Buy
1	Dog stem	¾" dia.	Use a ¾" dowel.
2	Dog cap	¼" x 1" x 1"	Plywood or hardwood
1 box	Wood screws	#6 x 1"	Wood screws

Tablesaw Workstation

The tablesaw is the go-to stationary tool in almost every shop, and with good reason: A tablesaw allows you to cut to size large sheet goods or hardwood stock. What's more, the cuts are quick, straight, and dead square. Outfitted with the proper jigs and accessories, your tablesaw can also cut a wide variety of joinery.

Benchtop tablesaws are relatively inexpensive machines, and they're a good choice for someone just getting started in woodworking. You can buy a stand with the saw, but you'll get more versatility by mounting your saw on a shopmade base. Building this solid, mobile unit for your benchtop saw not only provides a stable worksurface, it also increases the capacity of the saw to handle large workpieces.

The workstation offers a stable base, outfeed support, dust collection, and lots of storage. Built from ¾" plywood, this base has a wide-enough footprint to keep it from tipping as you work. It also offers outfeed support that allows you to cut long boards or sheet goods but folds out of the way when not in use. Just beneath the saw is a dust drawer to catch the bulk of the sawdust produced during cutting. A pair of storage drawers near the floor provides space for the tools you'll want close at hand. Add a few safety accessories and a crosscut jig, and you'll be amazed at what your tablesaw can do.

What You'll Learn

- Using biscuits to join a case piece
- Smart project assembly methods
- Building biscuited drawers
- Using safety accessories at the tablesaw
- Building jigs

Building this workstation is easy work, but it also teaches you some of the basics of woodworking: building and assembling a box. These same methods can be used for building cabinets, bookcases, even sideboards and chests of drawers. This workstation is put together using biscuits, which I prefer because they make it a lot easier for one person to manage all the parts, but

Work safer, get better results Smart techniques and the use of shopmade safety accessories are the keys to improving your skills.

Assembling a case piece Learn biscuiting techniques that will allow you to build sturdy boxes—the basic element of everything from chests of drawers to kitchen cabinets to storage chests.

screws and butt joints would do the same job. Once the base is built, you can set up the saw and begin using it. Outfeed support, as well as the storage and dust drawers, can be added at any time. That said, both the drawers and the outfeed support make this unit more stable and versatile, so I'd suggest building everything in one fell swoop.

You'll also learn the essentials of building and fitting drawers, as well as how to install a continuous hinge. And you'll get a little more practice with your plunge router, too. Once the base of the saw is built, you'll learn to use smart procedures for cutting, and build a number of accessories to make your work both safer and more precise.

A Versatile Workstation

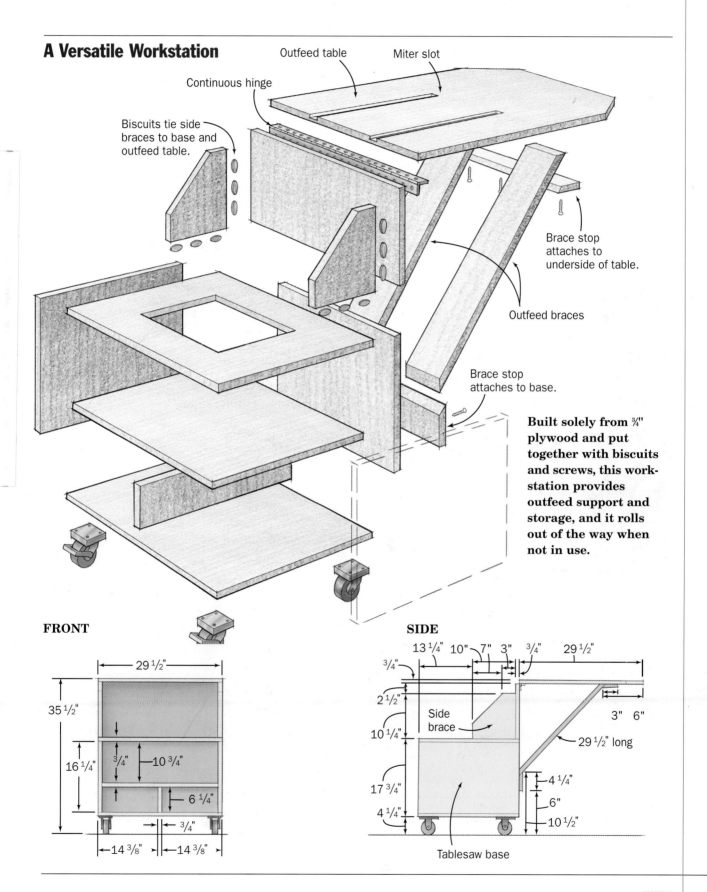

Outfeed table

Miter slot

Continuous hinge

Biscuits tie side braces to base and outfeed table.

Brace stop attaches to underside of table.

Outfeed braces

Brace stop attaches to base.

Built solely from ¾" plywood and put together with biscuits and screws, this workstation provides outfeed support and storage, and it rolls out of the way when not in use.

FRONT

29 ½"

35 ½"

16 ¼"

¾"

10 ¾"

6 ¼"

¾"

14 ⅜" 14 ⅜"

SIDE

13 ¼" 10" 7" 3" ¾" 29 ½"

¾"

2 ½"

Side brace

10 ¼"

3" 6"

29 ½" long

17 ¾"

4 ¼"

4 ¼"

6"

10 ½"

Tablesaw base

Quantity	Part	Actual Size	What to Buy
1	Top	¾" x 29½" x 24"	Use ¾" plywood. This project shows Baltic birch, but any hardwood plywood will do.
1	Bottom	¾" x 29½" x 24"	
2	Sides	¾" x 16¼" x 24"	
1	Shelf	¾" x 28" x 23¼"	
1	Divider	¾" x 6¼" x 23¼"	
1	Back	¾" x 16¼" x 28"	
2	Fixed casters	3½" wheels	Use heavy-duty casters with rubber wheels. The total height is 4¼".
2	Swiveling casters that lock	3½" wheels	Use heavy-duty casters with rubber wheels. Look for casters with a foot brake.
1 canister	Biscuits	#20	You'll need them for the drawers and the outfeed support.
1 box	Self-drilling screws	¾"	Use these to attach the casters.
16	Washers	¼" x ¾"	Use these to attach the casters.
	Lag screws	Sized to fit the holes in your tablesaw	If your tablesaw did not come with bolts and washers for attaching it to the top, you'll need lag screws.
	Misc.		A woodworking grade of yellow glue

Buying Materials

This entire project is can be built from two sheets of ¾" plywood, which can be found at any home center and most hardware stores. You can substitute MDF for the case and top, but stay away from it for the drawers, where you don't need the extra weight.

It's best to have the casters in hand before you begin building the box, because their height determines the height of the base. The casters used here are 4¼" tall and have heavy-duty rubber wheels; if you use 3¼" casters, add another inch to the height of the base. Aim for an overall height of around 35½". You can find casters through most mail-order supply houses (see Sources on p. 166.).

- ■ Circular saw
- ■ Straightedge guide for the circular saw
- ■ Benchtop tablesaw
- ■ Biscuit joiner
- ■ Jigsaw
- ■ Ratcheting screwdriver
- ■ Framing square
- ■ Straightedge
- ■ Combination square
- ■ Tape measure
- ■ Plunge router
- ■ ¾" x ¾" bearing-driven straight router bit
- ■ 1" chisel
- ■ Rubber mallet
- ■ Cordless drill/driver
- ■ ³⁄₁₆" drill bit
- ■ Countersink bit
- ■ Five 4'-long clamps
- ■ One 12'-long clamp
- ■ Socket wrench kit to attach the saw to the base (if using lag screws)
- ■ Miter gauge
- ■ Bandsaw or handsaw
- ■ Planer
- ■ Pencil for marking

Workstation

Before you start building the workstation, make sure the sizes shown in the drawing below work for your tablesaw model. This workstation is sized for one of the largest benchtop saws on the market, so it should handle whatever model you choose. But it's best to measure your saw and size the base accordingly, just in case.

The base should be about 4" wider than the base of your saw and 4" to 6" deeper than the saw table. Make sure there's enough room to accommodate your rip fence, as well as the anti-kickback fingers and splitter.

You may also have to make adjustments in the height of the box based on the casters you use (see "Buying Materials" on the facing page).

The base shown here can easily be sized to handle a larger contractor's saw. You'll have to remove the contractor's saw from its stock base—which usually means only removing four screws—but you'll wind up with a much more stable arrangement that provides needed outfeed support. The sturdy base will also help dampen the vibration you encounter on most contractor's saws.

Tablesaw Base

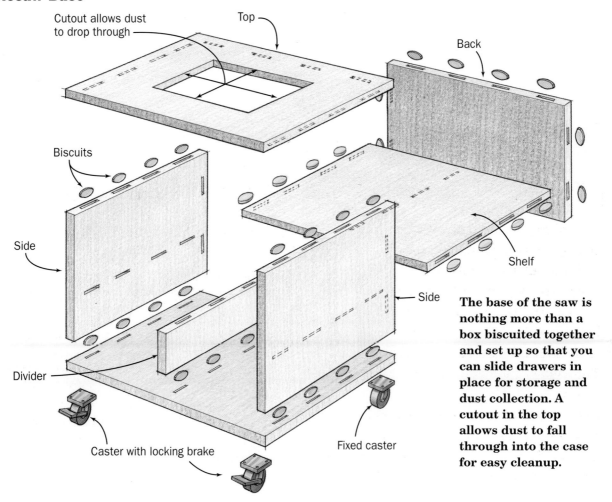

Cutout allows dust to drop through

Top

Back

Biscuits

Side

Shelf

Side

Divider

Caster with locking brake

Fixed caster

The base of the saw is nothing more than a box biscuited together and set up so that you can slide drawers in place for storage and dust collection. A cutout in the top allows dust to fall through into the case for easy cleanup.

Cut the Parts to Size

Once you confirm your measurements, mark them on the plywood. Then you're ready to cut the top, bottom, back, and sides to size.

1. First, clamp the plywood to a pair of saw-horses and cut it to a manageable size. It's easier to make the more precise cuts for width and length when you're not handling such large pieces. You can set up a straight-edge guide for your circular saw or simply mark a line and cut it freehand using the circular saw. Just be sure to leave an extra 1" or so on all sides to make it easier when trimming them to exact size.

2. Cut the pieces to the correct width and length using a circular saw and guide (see "A Shopmade Cutting Guide" on p. 19).

WORK SMART

When cutting multiple pieces to the same size, make all the cuts at the same time. For example, if you're cutting two boards to 30" by 30", cut one board to width—30" by 60"—then crosscut it in half to get the 30" length.

3. If you will be cutting a hole in the back of the base to accept a dust hose, go ahead and make that cut now, then cut the hole in the drawer later (see "Add Dust Collection" on p. 75). The hole can be anywhere at the top of the back of the base that will access the top drawer, and it should be the same size as the hose on your shop vacuum.

Cut the Joinery for the Case

TABLESAW SAFETY

To use a tablesaw safely, follow the guidelines here. And use your common sense. If something doesn't feel right, stop and check it out. Your instincts are probably right.

- Make sure the blade is never more than ⅛" above the workpiece.
- Never stand directly behind the sawblade when cutting.
- Don't back a workpiece out of a cut.
- Never cut freehand. Always use a fence, miter gauge, or crosscut sled.
- Use push sticks or paddles to keep stock against the fence and your hand away from the blade.

With the parts cut to size, you're ready to start the corner joinery. Simple butt joints screwed together will offer plenty of strength, but if you're working alone, using biscuits makes it a lot easier to position parts and hold them together while you get the clamps in place. If you've never used biscuits, try some practice runs and see "Skill Builder: Using a Biscuit Joiner" on p. 35.

1. While you've got the parts laid out, mark all of them so you'll know which piece goes where when you assemble the box (for more on this, see "The Cabinetmaker's Triangle" on the facing page).

2. For each corner joint, you'll be cutting biscuit slots in the face of one piece and the edge of its mate. To mark off locations for the biscuit slots, set each part in place and then mark centerlines for the biscuit slots, as shown in photo A. Don't try to dry-fit the whole case at once; simply hold adjoining parts together—one joint at a time—and mark the centerlines. There's no reason to get too fussy measuring out the placement of the biscuit— eyeballing it is fine. Just be sure to allow about 5" between each slot and distribute them evenly across the length of the joint.

Lay out the biscuit slots With the case parts set in place, use a combination square to mark out the centerlines for the biscuit slots.

THE CABINETMAKER'S TRIANGLE

The hardest part of building a box—be it a bookcase, chest, drawer, or this tablesaw unit—is often keeping all the parts straight. It's far too easy to confuse the side of a cabinet for the back, or the side of a nearly square drawer with the drawer front. This can cause big problems when it comes time to glue up.

An easy solution is to mark project parts using a technique called a cabinetmaker's triangle. Put simply, it's a triangle broken into four parts. By marking each workpiece with a part of the triangle, you'll be able to tell at a glance where the piece you're holding belongs. Mark the front edges of your workpieces so you'll know which edge faces the front and so you can easily see all the marks

when you're putting the project together. Bottoms of drawers or backs of cabinets can be marked with a full triangle. It's a handy and simple technique—all you need is a pencil—but it can save you lots of head-scratching and frustration.

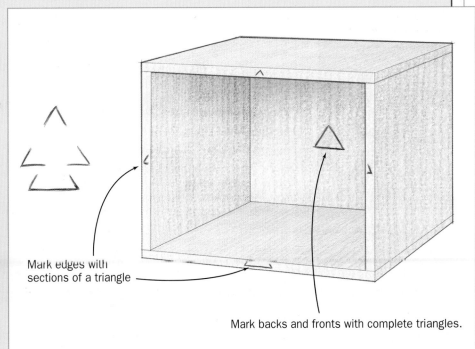

Mark edges with sections of a triangle

Mark backs and fronts with complete triangles.

B

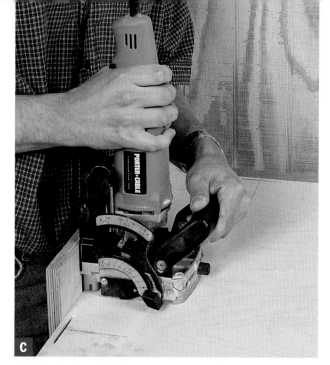

C

Biscuit the sides and back To biscuit along the edge of a board, secure the work, align the centerline on the workpiece with the centerline on the biscuit joiner, and plunge to make the cut.

Then biscuit the top and bottom With the work secured against a right angle—like your bench stop—hold the biscuit joiner against its edge, aligning the centerlines, and plunge to cut the biscuit slot.

3. To cut the slots in the edges of the plywood, lay the stock flat on the benchtop. I work against a bench stop to secure the workpiece in place, but you could also use clamps to secure it. Align the centerline of the biscuit joiner to the centerline on the workpiece, then plunge to make the cut, as shown in photo B. The fence on the biscuit joiner should either be removed or folded out of the way, depending on the design.

4. To cut the slots in the faces, butt the end of the stock against a right angle. If you've got a bench stop on your benchtop, it works great for this application. If not, simply clamp a board perpendicular to your worksurface. Then align the centerline of the biscuit joiner with the centerline of the workpiece and plunge to cut the slot, as shown in photo C.

Cut the Joinery for the Shelf and Divider

1. Instead of cutting the shelf to the size in the drawing, it's best to mark the size directly off the dry-fitted box, in case any small discrepancies were introduced. When you dry-fit the box, don't use any glue. Simply set the biscuits in place and use clamps to hold the assembly together. Once the base is clamped up, hold the shelf up to the case and mark it for cutting. Cut the shelf and make sure it fits, as shown in photo D.

WORK SMART

No matter what you're building, it's best to begin by measuring your first cuts according to the project plans. But once the exterior parts of a box have been cut, all other cuts can be marked to size directly from the partially assembled parts.

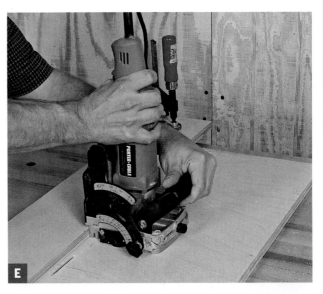

Be precise, stop measuring With the box partially assembled, mark out the shelf width and depth directly off the case rather than measuring with a tape measure. Here, the cut shelf is being set in place—it's a perfect fit.

Biscuit for the shelf Clamp the spacer to the edge of the side and position the biscuit joiner against it.

2. Cut the biscuit slots in the side edges of the shelf the same way you cut the edges in step 3 on the facing page. To complete the joints for the shelf, you need to cut biscuit slots in the middle of the side faces. To do this, mark the baseline of the shelf on the sides of the case while it is still clamped together. Mark biscuiting centerlines on the case with the shelf in place, then disassemble the case. Cut a spacer to the same height as the drawer opening. Then align the bottom edge of the spacer with the bottom edge of the case, clamp it in place, and you're ready to cut biscuits. Register the biscuit joiner against the spacer and align the biscuit joiner on the centerline, as shown in photo E. When you're done, save the spacer to use as the vertical divider.

3. Cut the spacer to the depth of the cabinet to make it a perfectly sized vertical divider.

4. Insert the divider into the case and mark the centerlines for the biscuit slots, as shown in photo F. Cut the biscuit slots in the edges

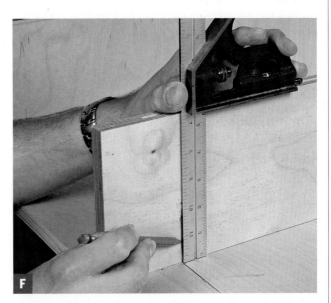

Mark the divider Set the divider in place on the shelf, then lay out centerlines for the biscuit slots. (Note that the case is upside down at this point.)

of the divider in the same way you cut the edges in step 3 on the facing page To complete the joints for the divider, you need to cut slots in the face of the shelf. To do so, follow the directions in step 2, above. Mark the baseline of the divider on the bottom of the shelf, then use a new spacer (aligned with the baseline on the divider) to hold the biscuit joiner in the correct position for cutting.

SKILL BUILDER: Assembling a Case Piece

What You'll Need

- **#20 Biscuits**
- **Glue**
- **Rubber mallet**
- **Clamps**
- **Tape measure**

The key to successful and stress-free glue-ups is to take a full dry run before you ever lay on the first drop of glue. That's the time to troubleshoot any kinks that might arise—while there's still time to remedy them—and a good way to make sure you have all the necessary clamps, mallets, and anything else you'll need once the glue goes on. It's also a good time to figure out the best order for assembling parts. Dry-fitting everything allows you to make sure that all the parts are aligned and the joints close up completely.

The photos in this section walk you though the assembling, gluing, and clamping processes on a biscuited case, but the procedures are the same for most rectilinear assemblies you'll run up against.

1. Preinstall all the biscuits, but don't glue them in yet.

2. Lay the largest piece—whether it is a side, bottom, or top piece—flat on a work-surface. (If it's a top, turn it upside down.) Use spacers beneath the assembly to hold it off the worksurface and accommodate clamps. The spacers should all be exactly the same thickness.

3. Install any pieces (in this case, sides and back) that stand upright off your base piece, as shown in photo A.

4. Slide in or otherwise fit in any horizontal case pieces, like shelves, as shown in photo B. If necessary, install additional uprights (like the dividers), as shown in photo C.

5. Fit the final piece onto the top of all the uprights, as shown in photo D. You may have to tap the top with a mallet. Once the joints are all aligned, the case should be fairly steady and square.

6. Set the clamps in place and tighten them. Make sure that the joints close up and that the front edges of the case are aligned flush to each other.

7. Loosen the clamps and disassemble the parts. With the clamps close by, retrace your steps, but put a small bead of glue in each joint before closing it, as shown in photo E.

8. Once the glue goes on, you'll need to move fast. Make sure the front edges of the shelf

and divider line up with the front edges of the sides, top, and bottom. Clamp the assembly as shown in photo F. The clamps should pull everything together, but if any joints won't close up, don't hesitate to pull them tight with a few drywall screws. The screws can be removed later if you don't like their look.

9. When all the clamps are installed and the joints closed up, measure diagonals across the front, as shown in photo G. If the two measurements are the same, the assembly is square. If not, add a clamp across the long diagonal and tighten it until both diagonal measurements are the same. Allow at least an hour of drying time before you remove the clamps.

Dry-Fit the Whole Assembly and Glue It Up

Once the biscuit slots are cut, it's tempting to glue up the assembly. You'll save yourself a lot of headaches, however, if you do a dry-fitting before any glue goes on. This is the time to figure out the order you will assemble the pieces and to make adjustments (see "Skill Builder: Assembling a Case Piece" on pp. 66–67).

For this piece, it's easiest to assemble the box upside down. Start with the top upside down on the benchtop, using a few spacers to hold it off the bench so you'll have room for the clamp heads. Make sure that all the biscuits are in place. Add the sides and back. Slide the shelf into place, then install the divider and bottom. You might need a mallet to gently tap the pieces into place. Once you're satisfied with the dry fit, take it all apart and reassemble it with glue.

Secure the Saw and Make It Mobile

Now it's time to create a cutout in the top of the base so that dust from the saw can fall through into the dust drawer. The size of the opening is not critical; just make sure you don't make it so large that the saw risks falling through. For this saw I allowed about a 5" inset from the edge of the base.

Unless you're sure that your saw will always live in one spot, adding casters is a good idea. With casters in place, you can easily roll the saw anywhere you need it or move it against a wall to store it out of the way. With the top cut out and the casters in place, you're ready to add the saw.

Make the cutout

1. Once you've determined the size of your hole, mark it on the top.

2. Drill access holes at the corners of the cutout so you can easily insert the jigsaw blade.

3. Slide the blade of your jigsaw through the hole at one corner. Cut from corner to corner, turning the saw at each corner to cut the adjacent side, as shown in photo H.

H

Cut out the top To allow dust to fall through into the base, make a cutout in the top. Drill access holes at the corners, then make the cut with a jigsaw.

4. Once the four sides are cut, you can touch up the corners with the jigsaw. But don't get too finicky—once the saw is installed, you'll never see this part of the base again.

Get rolling

Turn the base upside down so you can attach the casters. Put two fixed casters at the rear of the base and two locking, swiveling casters on the front, as shown in photo I. This arrangement will allow you to move the saw around, then lock it in place without walking around the saw or kneeling down to adjust levelers. Attach the casters inset about 1" from the edge of the base using washers and ¾" self-drilling screws, as shown in photo J.

I

Set the foot brake **For the front, you want casters that will lock in place easily, preferably with only foot pressure.**

J

Make it mobile **Install casters about 1" in from all four corners of the workstation.**

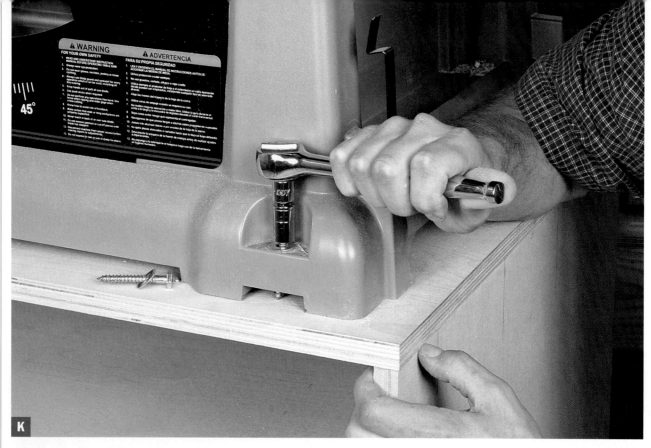

Secure the saw Secure the saw to the benchtop using lag screws, but don't overtighten them.

Attach the saw to the base

Most saws come with a set of bolts for attaching the top to a benchtop or a stand. If yours doesn't, secure it to the top using lag screws.

1. Set the saw in place on the base top, then mark through the bolt holes in the saw to locate the centers of the bolt holes on the top of the base.

2. With a drill bit roughly ¹⁄₁₆" larger in diameter than the bolts you'll use, drill holes at the locations you just marked. If you're using lag screws, the holes should be about ¹⁄₁₆" smaller in diameter than the lag screws.

3. Install the bolts and washers or the lag screws. If you use lag screws, be sure not to overtighten them, because you might crack the tablesaw case, as shown in photo K. If

the bolt's washers protrude into the bottom of the case, you'll need to cut away access slots in the back of the drawer to allow the drawer to slide by the washers. Do this when building the drawers (see "Cut the Parts to Size," step 2, on p. 79).

At this point, you can start using the saw, but the saw will be more efficient and safer if you add some kind of outfeed support on the rear side of the saw (see "Fold-Up Outfeed Table" on the facing page). Adding a dust-collection drawer underneath the saw (see "Drawers for Dust and Storage" on p. 79) will make for a much cleaner shop, but it won't affect the saw's usability for better or worse. Likewise, the storage drawers at the bottom of the saw come in handy around the shop, but they'll have no effect on the way the saw operates.

Fold-Up Outfeed Table

A tablesaw is a handy tool, but its usefulness increases greatly when you add proper outfeed support. You can use sawhorses or employ various other solutions for catching boards as they come off the blade when you're cutting, but they're often misaligned and cause more trouble than they prevent. Outfeed support that is too high is not just awkward, it's dangerous. Outfeed support that is too low is, well, not really outfeed support. It's worth taking some time to build this fold-up outfeed table. With only a hinge and some plywood, you can set up an outfeed table that is both stable and correctly aligned with the tablesaw table. What's more, when you're not using the saw, the outfeed table folds out of the way so that you can store the saw against a wall.

Make the Table

1. Cut the side braces to the right width and length at the tablesaw (see the drawing on p. 72).

2. Cut the rear outfeed support. Remember that your rear outfeed support must be ¾"

lower than the height of the tablesaw.

3. Cut the outfeed table on the tablesaw. The outfeed table can be just about any width you want, but I find it easiest to cut it to the same width as the rear outfeed support. With a

Fold-Up Outfeed Table

The outfeed table attaches to the back side
of the base using a continuous hinge so that
it will fold out of the way for easy storage.

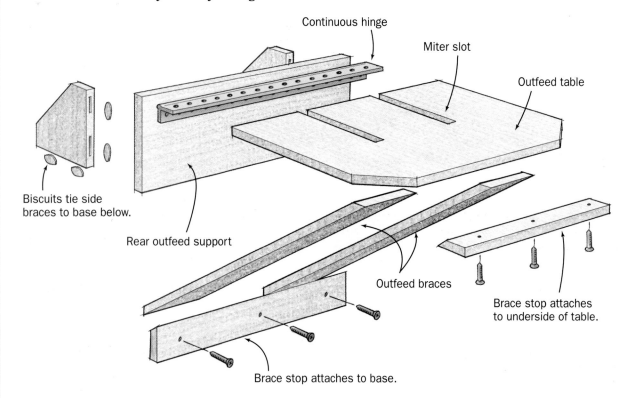

Continuous hinge

Miter slot

Outfeed table

Biscuits tie side
braces to base below.

Rear outfeed support

Outfeed braces

Brace stop attaches
to underside of table.

Brace stop attaches to base.

MATERIALS

Quantity	Part	Actual Size	What to Buy
1	Outfeed Table	¾" x 29½" x 29½"	Do not use pine plywood; the faces are too rough.
2	Brace stops	¾" x 4¼" x 27"	
2	Outfeed braces	¾" x 8" x 29½"	29½" overall length, with a 45° angle cut on one edge.
1	Continuous hinge	1½" x 24"	Use brass or steel. If you have to buy a longer hinge, you can trim it to length with a hacksaw.
2	Side braces	¾" x 10⅜" x 10"	
1	Rear outfeed support	¾" x 13" x 29½"	
	Biscuits	#20	You should have enough left over from the base.
1 box	Drywall screws	#6 x 1¾"	You'll only need a few, but it's best to buy a box and keep the extras at hand.
	Misc.		Yellow glue

Mark out biscuits for the braces Position the side braces, making sure to allow room for the rear support, and mark centerlines for biscuits on both the base and the braces.

Biscuit for the braces Using the upright support to position the biscuit joiner, cut the biscuit slots in the top of the base.

circular saw, cut 45° angles on the ends of the table to cushion any bumps against the edge.

4. Mark centerlines for the biscuit slots in the side braces and the base. Use a scrap of plywood as a spacer to inset the side braces ¾" from the back to accommodate the rear outfeed support, as shown in photo A. Clamp an upright support to the side of the base, then use it to register the base of the biscuit joiner as you plunge to make the cuts, as shown in photo B. Cut the biscuit slots in the braces by clamping them flat on the benchtop.

5. Set the biscuits in place on the base, glue the side braces to the base, and clamp them in place.

6. Glue the four biscuits into the horizontal faces of the side braces. Be sure to use only a little bit of glue, and don't allow it to drip onto the edge of the rear outfeed support. With the biscuits glued in place on the side brace, it is easier to adjust the rear outfeed support up or down so that you can level the

outfeed table with the tablesaw table, as shown in photo C.

7. Hold the rear outfeed support in place against the side braces and mark the centerlines for biscuits. Then butt the rear outfeed support against a 90° bench stop or another 90° support and cut the biscuit slots.

Preglue the biscuits to the rear support The biscuits on the side braces can be preglued into place, making it easier to shift this rear outfeed support up and down to the correct height.

Hinge the Table to the Brace

The rear outfeed support at the back of the saw is outfitted with a continuous hinge to support the outfeed table. It's best to install the hinge before you attach the rear outfeed support to the side braces.

1. At the workbench, lay the rear outfeed support and the table next to each other so the edges that will be hinged are against each other. Lay the hinge on top and install only about three screws into each side of the hinge—two at each end and another two near the center—until you're sure everything is aligned. Then install the remaining screws, as shown in photo D.

2. Set the hinged outfeed assembly in place on the back of the saw, using clamps to secure it.

3. Use a long straightedge or a combination square to check that the rear outfeed support is flush to the tablesaw table.

4. Adjust the clamps, if necessary, until the two surfaces line up. If there's any discrepancy, shift the rear outfeed support up or down on the biscuits installed in the side braces. The biscuits should allow enough wiggle room, but if not, you can relocate the hinge, widen the biscuit slots on the rear support, or trim off the bottom of the rear outfeed support. Don't permanently attach anything yet. You'll do that a little later (see "Attach the Outfeed Assembly to the Base" on p. 77).

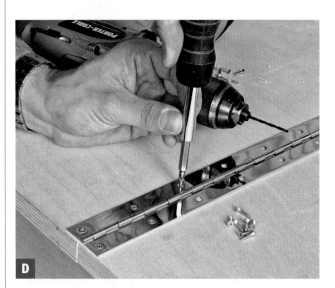

D Hinge the outfeed support **A continuous hinge attaches the outfeed table to the rear support. Screw it into place before installing the rear support to the base.**

E Keep it clean **To accommodate a saw with a dust-collection chute on the back, the rear outfeed support is cut out to accept a dust-collection hose. Start by drilling holes at the corners of the cutout, then make the cut with a jigsaw.**

ADD DUST COLLECTION

Adding dust collection to your tablesaw unit will keep your shop clean and alleviate some of the wear and tear that comes from your saw becoming clogged with dust. If you're using a saw with a dust chute on the rear side, you can cut an access hole in the rear outfeed support before assembly so you can attach your vacuum hose. After assembly, simply plug the hose into the dust chute to lower the amount of dust that winds up in the air and dust drawer.

Many benchtop saws don't have dust chutes, but you can easily add an access hole for your shop-vacuum hose through the side or back of the base and through the dust drawer (see the drawing below). There will still be dust in the drawer, but it won't fill up as quickly, and the suction from the hose will pull dust downward, away from the saw.

Fortunately, you can hook up almost any shop vacuum to both options. Some vacuums are "tool activated," meaning that you can plug the saw into the vacuum and the vacuum will switch on and off automatically when you turn your tablesaw on or off. Tool-activated vacuums are a little pricier than regular shop vacuums, but it's an option worth considering. I find that with a regular

Attach the vacuum On the saw used for this station, the vacuum hose attaches to the saw's dust chute through the cutout in the rear support.

shop vacuum, I often forget or don't bother to turn it on when I'm making quick cuts, and the mess starts creeping in.

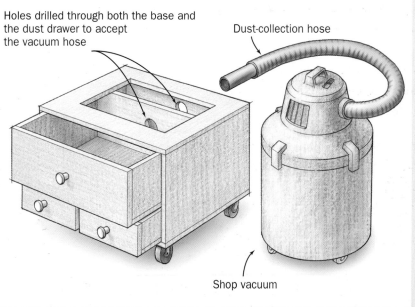

Holes drilled through both the base and the dust drawer to accept the vacuum hose

Dust-collection hose

Shop vacuum

5. If your saw has a dust chute at the rear of the saw, make a cutout in the rear outfeed support to access the dust-collection chute. Mark the location of the cutout hole on the rear outfeed support, then remove the rear outfeed support from the assembly. Make the cutout with a jigsaw. An oversized hole is fine for this configuration, so there's no reason to get too fussy measuring and cutting the hole. Simply drill holes to allow the jigsaw's blade to slide into place, and then make the cutout with a jigsaw, as shown in photo E. For more ideas on dust collection, see "Add Dust Collection" above.

Cut the Miter Slots

You'll need to cut grooves in the outfeed table to accommodate the miter gauge and any sleds you'll use for crosscutting. To do this, use a plunge router outfitted with a ¾" straight bit. The diameter of the bit is not critical—if you use a smaller bit, you'll just have to make more passes with the router.

1. If you've taken apart the assembly to add a dust-collection chute hole, you'll need to clamp the whole assembly to the side braces again. Slide the biscuits in place and tighten down the clamps so that the assembly won't shift.

2. Use a framing square to mark a line across from the saw's miter slots onto the outfeed table, as shown in photo F. You don't want the miter gauge to hit the sides of the groove, so mark lines about ¼" wider than

each side of the miter-gauge slot. That means the slots on your outfeed table will be about ½" wider than the slots on the table.

3. With the miter slots marked out, use a plunge router outfitted with a straight bit to make the cut for the miter gauge. Set the depth gauge on the router so that it allows you to cut a groove that is about ¹⁄₁₆" deeper than the miter slot on the tablesaw, and lock the plunge depth adjuster.

Rout the slots To cut the miter slots, run a plunge router outfitted with a straight bit against a straightedge clamped in place as a fence. Make one pass, adjust the fence, and then make another.

4. To cut the grooves, use a straightedge clamped to the workpiece as a fence. To align the fence, unplug the router and lower the bit until it just touches the workpiece. Set the edge of the bit against the mark denoting the edge of your groove at one end. Then butt the fence against the base of the router and clamp that end of the fence in place, as shown in photo G. Move the router to the other end, align the bit, and then clamp down that

Mark the miter slots Clamp the hinged rear outfeed support and outfeed table to the side braces, then mark out the miter slots on the outfeed table using a framing square. The miter slots should be wide and deep enough so that there's no risk of the miter gauge getting jammed when you make a cut.

end of the fence. Moving from left to right, take two or three passes with the router to reach the full depth of the slot.

5. Move the fence to the other side of the groove and align it as you did in step 4. Take passes with the router until you reach the correct depth. (Remember to rout in the opposite direction this time—handheld routing is always done left to right as you stand in front of the work.) For a cleaner look, you can square off the ends of the miter slots with a chisel. Repeat the process to cut the other miter slot.

Attach the Outfeed Assembly to the Base

Once the hinge is installed and the miter slots have been cut, you're ready to attach the outfeed table assembly to the side braces on the base.

1. Apply glue to the rear outfeed support and to the biscuits on the side braces. Attach the outfeed assembly to the side braces and clamp the assembly together. Use a straightedge to help position the top of the outfeed table so that it's flush with the tablesaw table, and make any adjustments quickly, before the glue cures, as shown in photo H. To free up your hands, use a sawhorse when aligning the end of the outfeed table, adding enough scraps of plywood to bring it flush to the tablesaw surface. The sawhorse also supports the table while the glue dries.

2. Once you've got the height of the outfeed table, tighten down the clamps and add a few drywall screws through the rear outfeed support into the side braces, as shown in photo I.

Test the height When attaching the outfeed table to the tablesaw unit, clamp it in place and test the height against the tablesaw table with a straightedge.

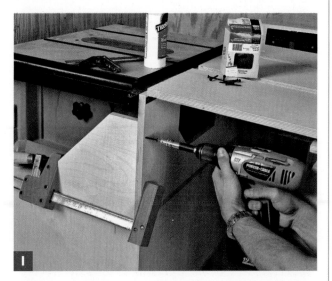

Attach the rear support Once the outfeed table is aligned, tighten the clamps and add a few drywall screws to pull the tops of the joints closed.

WORK SMART

Biscuit slots leave a bit of room so that you can make minor realignments before the outfeed table is attached. For even more flexibility, make a few separate cuts with the biscuit joiner to both the right and left of the biscuiting centerline.

Cut and Install the Outfeed Braces

Unless your tablesaw is going to live in one spot, being able to fold the outfeed table down and out of the way will come in handy, as shown in photo J. But to support the table, you should add one or two removable braces that span from the base to the outfeed table. This project uses two, but if you use only one brace, cut it about 6" wider than those shown in the chart on p. 72.

1. Cut the brace stops that support the outfeed braces. At the tablesaw, cut two lengths of plywood to width. Then crosscut a 45° angle on one edge. To set the blade of your tablesaw to 45°, crank the adjuster on the side of the saw. To dial in the exact angle, hold a combination square against the table and flush to the side of the blade.

2. Attach the brace stops to the back of the base and to the underside of the outfeed table using drywall screws. Make sure that they are attached at equal distances from the hinge.

Fold the table down When not in use, remove the braces to fold the table down and out of the way.

3. Once the brace stops are in place, cut the braces themselves. Use a miter gauge to crosscut 45° angles on both ends of each brace. It's best to cut the braces a little long at first, then slowly trim them at the tablesaw, testing their fit against the brace stops between cuts, as shown in photo K.

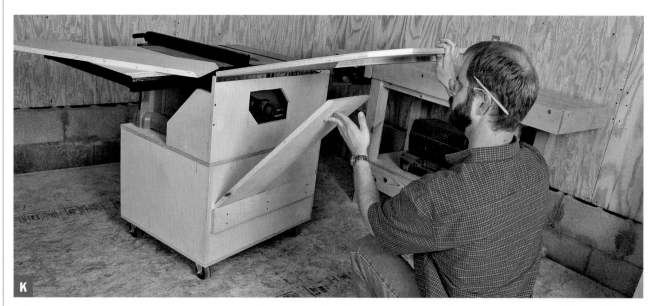

Raise the outfeed table To use the outfeed table, simply raise the table and slide the mitered braces into place. To add the first brace, lift the top and lower it onto the brace. Then add the second brace by sliding it in from the side.

Drawers for Storage and Dust Collection

Drawer joinery comes in many forms, but there's no reason to spend too much time outfitting this unit with fancy joinery. Plain plywood biscuited together is more than sufficient in this application, and the added weight of plywood only makes the base more stable.

But building these drawers is also a good primer for understanding basic drawer construction. You can get as tricky as you want, but a drawer is really nothing more than a box that fits inside a slightly larger box. Why complicate it?

Quick Drawers with Biscuits

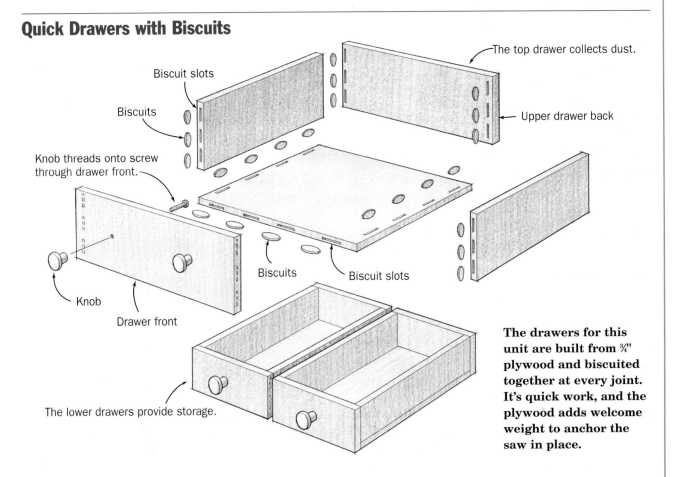

Biscuit slots

Biscuits

Knob threads onto screw through drawer front.

Knob

Drawer front

Biscuits

Biscuit slots

The top drawer collects dust.

Upper drawer back

The lower drawers provide storage.

The drawers for this unit are built from ¾" plywood and biscuited together at every joint. It's quick work, and the plywood adds welcome weight to anchor the saw in place.

Cut the Parts to Size

1. Start by cutting all your stock to size. Size the drawer fronts first, testing the size directly off the front of the case instead of using the measurements in the drawings on p. 59. You

don't want the fit to be too tight, or the drawer will get jammed as you remove it. Aim for a ¹⁄₁₆" gap on all sides, as shown in photo A on p. 80. The easiest way to check

Size the drawer front You'll want about a ¹/₁₆" gap on all sides of the drawer front.

the gap is to set the front in the drawer opening flat against one side and the bottom, then make sure you've got a ⅛" gap at the top and on the other side. The back should be cut to exactly the same size as the drawer front.

Test the height The surest way to gauge the height for the drawer sides is to slide them in place.

MATERIALS

Quantity	Part	Actual Size	What to Buy
1	Upper drawer front	¾" x 10" x 28"	
2	Upper drawer sides	¾" x 10" x 21½"	
1	Upper drawer back	¾" x 10" x 28"	
1	Upper drawer bottom	¾" x 27½" x 21½"	
2	Lower drawer fronts	¾" x 6¼" x 13¾"	
4	Lower drawer sides	¾" x 6¼" x 21¾"	
2	Lower drawer backs	¾" x 6¼" x 13¾"	
2	Lower drawer bottoms	¾" x 13¾" x 21½"	
4	Drawer pulls		Any kind is fine. We used inexpensive wooden pulls for this project.
	Biscuits	#20	You should have enough left over from the base.
1 box	Drywall screws		
	#6 x 1¾"		You should have enough left over from the outfeed table.
	Misc.		Yellow glue

2. If your tablesaw is bolted (rather than screwed) to the case, you can either make small cutouts in the drawer back that allow it to pass by the washer, or simply cut the back narrow enough so that it doesn't get stuck on the washers. If you've added a hole for dust collection to the back of the base, then make a matching hole in the back of the drawer. To mark the hole, set the back of the drawer in the drawer opening, then mark the hole directly off the hole on the base.

3. Size the drawer sides directly off the base, as shown in photo B. Place a spacer the thickness of the drawer bottom below the sides as you test their size. And remember that the drawer front and back need to be added, so the side should end 1¾" from the front. You want a fit that is loose but not sloppy, so allow about a ⅟₁₆" to ⅛" gap at the top.

4. Size the bottom so that it's the same width as the drawer front and 1¾" shy of the full depth of the opening. This allows room for the front and back to be mounted on the edge of the drawer bottom. It also allows enough room for the drawer fronts to be recessed about ¼" from the front of the face when closed.

Cut the Joinery and Glue It Up

At this point, you're ready to start cutting biscuit slots to joint all the edges of the drawers. You've done a lot of biscuiting already, but if you need to review it in more detail, see "Skill Builder: Using a Biscuit Joiner" on p. 35 in the Workbench chapter. Remember to mark all the drawer parts with a cabinetmaker's triangle to keep track of the loose parts, as shown in photo C (see "The Cabinetmaker's Triangle" on p. 63).

1. Hold the parts in place and mark center-lines for biscuits on all the mating parts.

C

Mark parts clearly Set all the parts in place and mark mating boards with centerlines to locate the biscuit joiner for cutting slots. Note the cabinetmaker's triangle on the top edges of the drawers. It will help you keep the parts in the right place as you cut joinery.

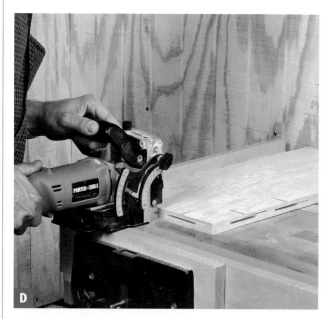

Work off a flat reference surface Where edges are slotted for biscuits, set the biscuit joiner flat on the benchtop and align it with the centerlines.

Biscuit the drawers As you did for the top of the base, biscuit the faces of the drawer pieces using the benchtop as a right-angle jig.

Assemble the dust drawer With the drawer sides in place, slide the front and back into position.

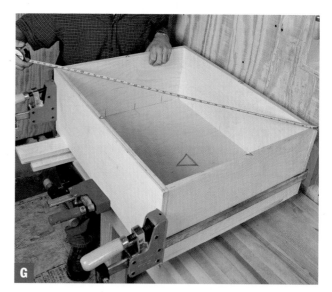

Clamp up the drawer Check to see that the assembly is square by measuring both diagonals—they should be the same.

2. Cut all of the biscuits in the edges, as shown in photo D, and then use a 90° stop to cut the biscuit slots on the faces, as shown in photo E. Continue until you've biscuited all the drawer pieces.

3. Do a full dry-fitting, as shown in photo F.

When you clamp up the drawer, you should be able to hold it together with only a few clamps running from front to back, as shown in photo G. You only need to apply enough clamps to make sure the joints close up. And be sure to work on a flat surface. After a full dry-fitting, you're ready to glue up.

The Polishing Touches

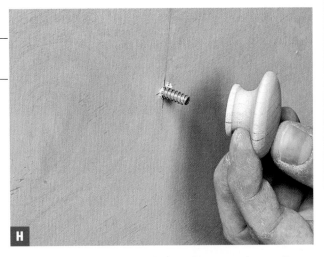

O nce the drawers have been built, it's time to add the drawer pulls. For wooden knobs, just drill holes, sink the screws from inside the drawers, and screw the knobs down on the screws, as shown in photo H.

Finishing the tablesaw unit is not necessary, but put at least a coat of wax on the bottoms and sides of the drawers so they open and close smoothly. Whatever you do, don't put a thick top coat, like polyurethane or varnish, on the sides or insides of the drawers. The little bit of extra thickness can cause the drawers to jam. In fact, steer clear of using oil-based finish on the insides of the drawers altogether—the smell never goes away. If you really want to finish the insides of the drawers, use a light coat of shellac.

Attach pulls **Wooden pulls are inexpensive and easily installed. Simply drill a hole, insert the screw from inside the drawer front, then screw the knob onto the screw.**

Now you're ready to start using the drawers. Thanks to the dust drawer, you will be able to get rid of dust quickly, as shown in photo I, and you'll have plenty of storage.

Keep a clean shop **After a day of heavy work, the dust drawer can be removed and emptied into the trash.**

Using the right safety accessories can not only help prevent accidents but also make your work more precise. All of these accessories allow you to apply leverage at the crucial moment when you realize that your hand is too close to the blade. The result is a straighter cut, less anxiety, and a more rewarding day in the shop—not to mention a hand with all of its fingers intact.

Push Sticks, Push Shoes, and Push Paddles

Push sticks and push shoes are handy for ripping narrow stock, but use a push paddle whenever the width of the board allows. Push paddles offer better control over the stock (see the photo at right). Whether you're cutting wide stock or ripping thin strips, position the accessory to keep the stock against the fence. This often means that the push stick or push paddle runs directly through the blade. Just make sure you never raise the blade more than ⅛" above the top of the stock you're cutting.

Zero-Clearance Insert

The throat plate that comes with a tablesaw is made to accommodate cuts ranging from 90° to 45°. It's fine for many applications, but when you are removing thin offcuts, the opening is so wide that it allows them to get jammed. For these procedures, you'll need a zero-clearance insert that leaves no gap between the blade and the insert.

To ready the insert for use, lower the blade on your saw and set the insert in place. Clamp a length of 2x4 to the tablesaw over the top of the insert, then flip the saw on and slowly raise the blade (see the

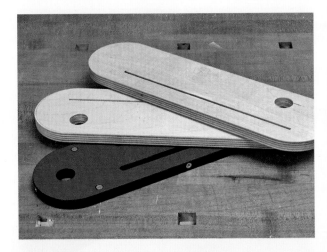

bottom photo above). Just make sure the stock is thick enough to keep the blade from cutting it in half. You can flip the same insert end for end and repeat the process to accommodate angled or dado cuts, or use a fresh insert. Either way, set up the dado or angled blade arrangement, lower the blade, and repeat the process of raising the blade.

Featherboards

Clamped securely to the tablesaw and against the stock you're cutting, featherboards ensure that your workpiece stays flush against the rip fence (see the photos above). And if a board does manage to drift away from the fence, the teeth of a featherboard help prevent the workpiece from kicking back toward you. You can make your own with a handsaw or buy an aftermarket version.

Crosscut Box

Crosscut sleds Sleds make easy work of handling long or wide stock that can be difficult to crosscut with a miter gauge alone.

Miter gauges can handle crosscutting small or short stock, but for large workpieces like shelves or a tabletop, a sliding crosscut sled works much better. Making one takes only a few hours, a quarter of a sheet of plywood, and a few scrap pieces of hardwood. A crosscut sled has a flat plywood bed that rides on the table of your tablesaw. The bed is guided by two runners that ride in the miter slots. On the front of the sled, you attach a fence that is perfectly square to the tablesaw blade,

and on the back you add a rear fence to keep the bed from coming apart as you cut.

When it's time to make a cut, simply slide the sled into place on your saw, then drop the workpiece into position and run it through the blade. You can make crosscut sleds in various sizes and add attachments for making repeating cuts to exactly the same length or for cutting miters, tenons, or even dadoes.

Crosscut Sled

A crosscut sled allows you to make cuts that you can't manage with a miter gauge alone.

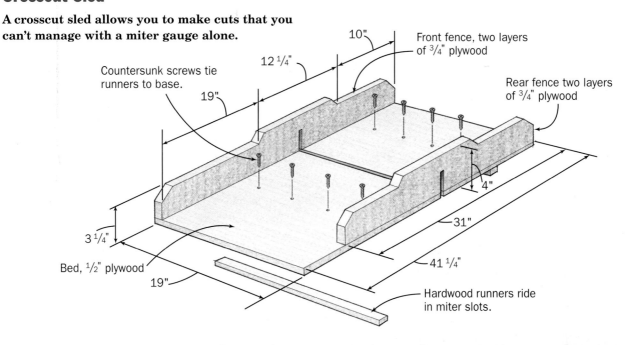

Countersunk screws tie runners to base.

Front fence, two layers of ¾" plywood

Rear fence two layers of ¾" plywood

10"

12¼"

19"

4"

31"

3¼"

41¼"

Bed, ½" plywood

19"

Hardwood runners ride in miter slots.

MATERIALS			
Quantity	Part	Actual Size	What to Buy
1	Base	½" x 41¼" x 19"	¼ sheet of ½" plywood
2	Runners	¼" x ¾" x 19"	Use a hardwood like maple or oak.
2	Front fence	¾" x 4" x 41¼"	
2	Rear brace	¾" x 4" x 31"	
8	Steel wood screws	½"	
1 box	Drywall screws	#6 x 1¼"	You'll only need a few, but it's best to buy a box and keep the extras at hand.
	Misc.		Yellow glue

Attach the Runners to the Bed

1. Cut the bed to size with either your table-saw or a circular saw and a straightedge guide. In theory, you can build sleds as large as you'd like, but in practice, it becomes awkward when they're much larger than the top of your saw.

2. Cut the runners to length, then run the stock through a benchtop planer until it's

WORK SMART

If the runners are tight in the grooves, use a mill file with a "safe" (dull) edge to trim them to size. To determine which parts need filing, rub pencil lead in the miter slot, then run the sled through it. File off the portions of the runners that are marked with lead.

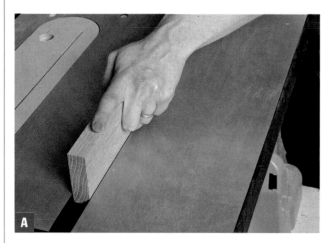

Plane the runners to size Use a benchtop planer to thickness a length of stock until it fits in the miter slot.

Find a good fit Rip the runners to size on the tablesaw, and then check their fit in the miter slots.

thin enough to ride in the miter slots smoothly, as shown in photo A. The fit should be snug but loose enough so that the runners can still move freely back and forth. If you don't have a planer, you can buy metal versions of the runners from any mail-order woodworking outlet (see Sources, p. 166).

3. Cut the board widthwise twice, creating runners that are a hair shallower than the depth of the miter slot. When laid flat, they should be just below the top of the tablesaw, as shown in photo B.

4. To attach the bed to the runners, square the bed against the tablesaw fence. Predrill holes, set the runners in place, and then screw through the bed into them, as shown in photo C. Use short, ½" screws, and be sure to

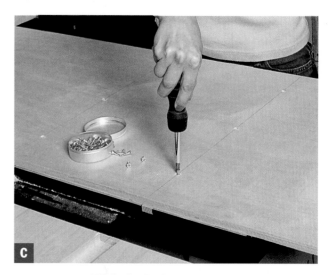

Add the bed With the bed squared up against the tablesaw fence, screw through the top of the jig and into the runners.

countersink the heads. If the runners don't slide smoothly, you can still make a few adjustments (see "Work Smart" on p. 87).

Attach the rear fence

1. The front and rear fences are each made with two pieces of plywood glued and screwed together. Cut the fences. The length of the rear fence is not important, but the height should be the same as the front fence. Put a thin layer of glue on each piece, and then join each set of pieces together and reinforce with

drywall screws. You can either remove the screws after the glue dries, or position them so that the tablesaw blade won't run into one. The exact location of the screws isn't important as long as they don't interfere with the blade.

2. Once the glue has dried, use a jigsaw to shape the tops of the fences.

3. Set the rear fence in place and clamp it to the bed. Put the bed upside down on a flat surface, then drive a few drywall screws through the bottom of the bed into the rear fence.

4. Once the rear fence is attached, you need to create a kerf line to square the front fence to. Raise the blade on the saw and cut about halfway through the bed, as shown in photo D. Then reach down and turn off the saw before completing the cut. Keep a good hold on the sled until the blade stops running.

Attach the front fence

1. The front fence is used as a reference surface for cutting stock, so it needs to be perfectly square to the blade. Set the front fence in place. Hold a framing square against the kerf you just cut and the front fence, and align, as shown in photo E.

2. Use a pair of clamps to secure the fence, and then make small adjustments if necessary.

3. Once the fence is square, tighten the clamps and turn the bed upside down. Then drive in a few screws through the bottom into the fence, as shown in photo F.

4. Make a number of test cuts and check the results with a combination square. If further adjustments need to be made, remove the screws from the front fence and realign.

E

Locate the front fence **Place one arm of a framing square against the kerf left by the tablesaw cut and align the fence to the other arm, then clamp it in place.**

F

Attach the fence **Drywall screws tie the front fence to the bed of the sled. Don't glue it in place in case you need to make adjustments in the future.**

D

Cut halfway through the base **With the runners riding in the miter slots, run the sled through the saw until you've cut halfway though.**

Router Table

A router is among the most versatile tools in a workshop. You can use it to profile edges and to cut dadoes, grooves, and countless other types of joinery. Building a router table makes many routing tasks safer and easier, and it opens the door to a host of applications that simply can't be done with a handheld router.

A router table is really nothing more than a router inverted under a worksurface so that the bit protrudes through the top. Instead of passing the router over the work—as you would with handheld routing—you pass the work over the exposed, rotating bit.

A router table does not have to be elaborate (see "A Quick Router Table" on p. 99). The router table built in this chapter is no-nonsense, but it does everything a commercial router table will do at a fraction of the price. The base is nothing more than a plywood box with a pair of drawers added for storage. The top is glued up from two pieces of MDF. With a little wax, the top is just as smooth as a laminated commercial version.

You'll use a router table to cut dadoes and grooves, raise panels for cabinet doors, and profile edges, but this is just the beginning of what a router table can do. With time, you'll learn to cut various patterns using templates and guides, and a countless number of jigs and fixtures can be used in conjunction with a router table to cut specialized joinery.

What You'll Learn

- **Cutting dadoes and rabbets at the tablesaw**
- **Edging plywood with hardwood trim**
- **Cutting dadoes and rabbets at the router table**
- **Using dowels to peg joints**
- **Construction of a traditional drawer**
- **Safe techniques at the router table**

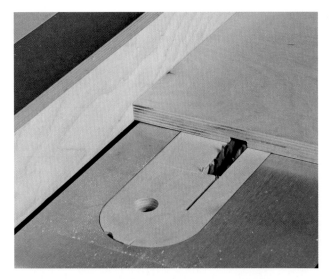

Cut dadoes and grooves Learn to use a dado set to cut dadoes, grooves, and rabbets at the table saw.

This is a very traditional version of a router table, complete with storage drawers and a versatile fence system, but it's also very straightforward to build. Instead of using biscuits to assemble the basic case, as you've done in earlier projects, you'll learn to cut dadoes and rabbets to construct a case piece. Once you've built this base, you'll understand the basics of cabinetmaking, a skill that will come in handy for multiple projects around the shop or house.

This project calls for two storage drawers. The traditional methods used for building the drawers can be applied to drawers of any size. Once you master this skill, you can add drawers to pretty much any other case piece. The corners of the drawers can be nailed together, but using pegs to join them lends a cleaner look.

With this project, you'll have a chance to practice various other tasks involved in woodworking. The front edges of the base are trimmed with hardwood, which lends nothing in terms of usability, but does give the piece a cleaner look. You can use this same method on bookcases, cabinets, or any number of furniture pieces.

Trim plywood The raw edges of plywood can be trimmed with hardwood strips to disguise plywood as hardwood.

Shopmade Router Table

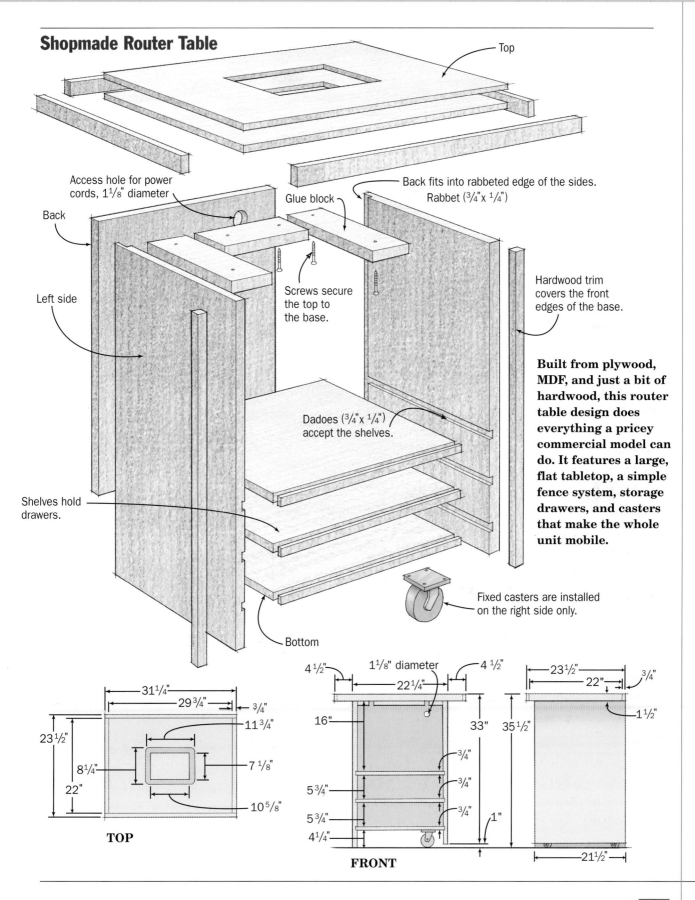

Top

Access hole for power cords, 1⅛" diameter

Back

Glue block

Back fits into rabbeted edge of the sides.
Rabbet (¾"x ¼")

Screws secure the top to the base.

Left side

Hardwood trim covers the front edges of the base.

Built from plywood, MDF, and just a bit of hardwood, this router table design does everything a pricey commercial model can do. It features a large, flat tabletop, a simple fence system, storage drawers, and casters that make the whole unit mobile.

Dadoes (¾"x ¼") accept the shelves.

Shelves hold drawers.

Fixed casters are installed on the right side only.

Bottom

TOP

31¼"
29¾"
¾"
11¾"
23½"
8¼"
7⅛"
22"
10⅝"

FRONT

4½"
1⅛" diameter
22¼"
4½"
16"
33"
35½"
¾"
5¾"
¾"
5¾"
¾"
1"
4¼"

23½"
22"
¾"
1½"
21½"

MATERIALS

Quantity	Part	Actual Size	What to Buy
1	Left side	¾" x 21¼" x 34"	All base and fence parts can be cut from a single sheet of ¾" plywood.
1	Right side	¾" x 21¼" x 33"	Cut to final length only after cutting joinery.
3	Shelves	¾" thick x 20½" deep x 21¼" wide	
1	Back	¾" x 21¼" x 33"	
3	Glue blocks	2" x 15"	Use scrap plywood.
6	Drywall screws	1½"	
1	Trim for right side	¾" x ¼" x 33"	All the trim is cut from hardwood stock.
1	Trim for left side	¾" x ¼" x 33¾"	
3	Trim for shelves	¾" x ¼" x 20¾"	
2	Fixed casters	4¼" tall	They do not need to swivel or lock.
16	Wood screws	¾"	Make sure that your screws are short—no more than ¾"—so that they won't protrude through the stock and impede the action of the drawer.
2	Top	¾" x 22" x 29¾"	MDF
1	Router insert	11¾" x 8¼"	If you buy a different size insert, adjust measurements on the top as needed.
4	Machine screws with countersunk heads	Sized to fit your particular router	If they weren't in your router set, pick up a few screws long enough to reach through the insert and into the base. When shopping for them, bring your router base and test their fit before you take them home.
2	Front and back trim for top	¾" x 1½" x 31¼"	Choose straight, knot-free boards.
2	Side trim for top	¾" x 1½" x 23½"	
2	Drawer fronts	¾" x 5¾" x 20¾"	
4	Drawer sides	½" x 5¾" x 20¾"	¼ sheet is enough to cut all the drawer sides.
2	Drawer backs	½" x 20¼" x 20¼"	¼ sheet will give you both pieces.
2	Drawer bottoms	¼" x 20¼" x 19¾"	Both can be cut from ¼ sheet of ¼" plywood.
1	Dowel	⅛" diameter	Cut into 1½" sections to make pegs.
2	Drawer knobs		Wooden ones are fine.
4	Biscuits	#20	
4	Fence support blocks	3" x 3"	Use ¾" sheet goods.
1	Fence face	¾" x 4" x 35"	MDF works as well as plywood in this application.
1	Fence base	¾" x 4" x 35"	
	Finishing nails	1½"	
	Misc.		Yellow glue, shellac, wax

Buying Materials

Most of the supplies for this router table can be bought at the local home center or hardware store. The base of this project is built from ¾" plywood. I used Baltic birch, but you could use a less expensive grade of birch, oak, or even pine. Whatever you choose, buy a length of hardwood that matches the color of your plywood to trim the edges of the plywood, and make sure you buy enough to trim out the top as well.

The MDF used on the top can be cut from a full sheet, but most large home centers also sell it by the half or quarter sheet. Two quarter sheets or one half sheet is all you'll need.

You'll also want to buy a router insert. Many home centers sell them, but mine came from Bench Dog Tools® (see Sources on p. 166). I prefer the relatively small size of the Bench

Dog Tools and similar inserts because they're less prone to sag over time.

Shopmade Router Table

The base is nothing more than a plywood box with drawers installed. It also features casters on one side of the base, so it's easy to move your table around the shop. The mobility comes in handy when you have to accommodate long or curved stock, or are ready to store the table against a wall and out of the way. Many commercial versions also feature doors at the top of the cabinet, but I've always found them more of a hindrance than a help because you're constantly opening and closing them to adjust the height of the bit. But if you'd like doors, you can add them later.

It's a good idea to buy your router insert before you decide on the size of the top. The size of the top is not critical, but you must have enough room to accommodate the insert. You should also make sure that the top overhangs the sides of the base by a few inches on each side so that you're able to clamp the fence securely in place.

I've designed this router table to be the same height as both the workbench and the tablesaw workstation. At this height, you can push it alongside your workbench to provide more worksurface, or alongside the tablesaw to provide additional outfeed support on the left side. If your workbench and tablesaw are a little taller or shorter, adjust your measurements accordingly.

Building the Base

The base of this router table is a simple box that is dadoed and rabbeted together. It includes shelves that serve as runners for two plywood drawers. The bottom of the case is shorter on the right side and on the back to accommodate two casters. The casters are all you need to make the whole assembly mobile.

Size the plywood

1. To make the plywood parts easier to handle around the shop, set the plywood atop sawhorses and cut the large parts to rough size using your circular saw.

2. Use a circular saw and guide to trim the sides and back to the correct height (see "A Shopmade Cutting Guide" on p. 19). Some tablesaws can make this cut, but most benchtop versions don't offer a wide-enough clearance between the fence and the blade. Handling such a large piece of stock can be awkward anyway, so trimming it to height with a circular saw is often the best option.

3. Trim the shelves and back all to the same width at the tablesaw.

4. Move the fence in ¾", and then trim the shelves to the correct depth.

Cut the joinery

1. Use a tape measure to mark out the bottom and the shelf locations on one side of the base.

2. Outfit the tablesaw with a dado set sized to ¾" wide and raise the blade for a ¼"-deep cut. Take a few passes on test stock to make sure that the dado is the right size. Test-fit by sliding a piece of ¾" plywood into the dado. A well-fitted dado will hold the mating stock upright, but it shouldn't be so tight that it takes a mallet to set it in place.

3. Line up the first shelf mark on the side with the blade, then adjust the fence to guide the cut accordingly, as shown in photo A. When making the cut, be sure to keep the face flat on the table. Using a push paddle helps keep downward pressure on the stock.

Dado the sides Before cutting, take a few test passes on scrap to make sure the width of the dado matches the width of the shelves. On smaller saws, limiting the depth of cut to ¼" should prevent the saw from bogging down.

Cut the corresponding dado on the other side before adjusting the fence.

4. To cut the rabbets on the back edges of the sides, run the fence all the way up to the edge of the dado blade. Be sure you use an auxiliary fence and lock it in place. Remember to keep the face flat on the table as you cut, as shown in photo B.

5. Once all the joinery is cut, trim about 1" off the bottom of the right side to make it the same length as the back of the case. The shorter side and back will allow you to lift up the left side of the router table and wheel the unit around the shop.

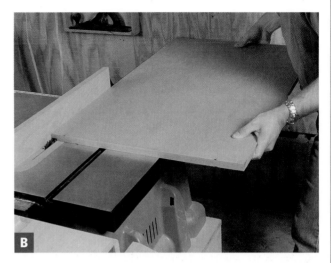

A rabbet is a dado at the edge A rabbet is nothing more than a dado cut along the edge of a board. Keep the stock flat on the tablesaw table to ensure a cut of consistent depth.

Assemble the base

Even the simplest of glue-ups can become harried affairs, but they don't have to be. Avoid the confusion by doing a run-through of the process before you add even one drop of glue. You'll even want to clamp up the assembly to make sure all the joints close up. When you disassemble the dry-fitted case, keep all the clamps close at hand for glue-up.

1. Start by laying one side flat on a pair of sawhorses, with the dadoes face up.

2. Apply a bead of glue in each dado. Applying glue in the dado rather than on the shelves prevents dripping glue from making a mess of your project. Then set the shelves in place, as shown in photo C.

3. Apply a bead of glue to the edges of the shelves, then set the side atop them, as shown in photo D on p. 98. Tap the side with a rubber mallet to make sure the joints are tight all the way across their length.

Set the shelves in place With one side of the base flat on sawhorses, fit shelves into the dados.

4. Use clamps to pull the assembly closed, as shown in photo E on p. 98, but slide the back into place before you tighten them completely, as shown in photo F on p. 98. Having the back in place before you tighten the clamps ensures that the whole assembly is square. Be sure the fronts of the shelves are flush with the sides.

Add the second side Glue the second side in place, then give it a few raps with a rubber mallet to make sure the shelves bottom out in the dadoes.

Clamp it up Apply clamps across the front and back of the assembly. Before you tighten down the clamps, be sure the front edges of the shelves are flush to the sides.

5. Once the clamps are tightened, measure across the diagonals at the front and back. But remember to measure from the bottom of the lower shelf, not from the bottom of the sides (because one side is shorter than the other). Equal measurements mean the assembly is square. If it's slightly off, check to see that the clamps are all aligned parallel to the shelves. If you still have trouble, apply clamps diagonally across the front and tighten them until you get equal measurements across the diagonals.

Slide the back in place Before tightening the clamps on the rear side, slide the back into the rabbeted sides. Installing the back now helps ensure that the assembly goes together square.

Attach the casters

When the clamps come off—you should give the glue at least an hour to dry—it's time to make the unit mobile. Installing fixed casters that don't spin enables you to wheel the router table around the shop.

1. Set your casters in place at the two right-hand corners of the router-table base. Align them so that the wheels are as far apart as possible and are parallel to the front of the base.

2. Mark the centerpoints of the screw holes in the casters with an awl. Then remove them and predrill the bottom shelf with a bit just under the size of the screws you're using.

3. Set the casters in place and screw them in.

While it's nice to have a freestanding, dedicated router table, it's quick work to make a simplified version out of scrap lumber you have lying around the shop. I built this design when I was visiting my father years ago and was helping him build a table. It was just a quick fix for the task at hand, but after five years it's seen tons of work and has never let him down. A scrap of lumber does a good job as a fence.

1. Start by cutting the tabletop to size at the tablesaw. The size is not critical, but 10" x 15" is about the minimum, and anything larger than 20" x 20" is likely to sag over time.

2. Cut 2x4 stock to the width of the top, then screw it in place, making sure the screw heads are fully countersunk. This is the arm, which you'll use to clamp the router table into your bench vise.

3. Drill the access hole for a router bit using a large drill bit (1¼" or larger).

4. Locate the router on the underside of the top, then attach it to the table using the same methods outlined for mounting a router to an insert (see photos on pp. 109–110).

Once built, this design can be stored easily out of the way. If possible, leave the router base mounted to the plywood. When needed, simply clamp the 2x4 arm into the vise on your workbench. If you're without a vise, skip attaching the 2x4 arm and simply clamp the top to hang off a flat worksurface.

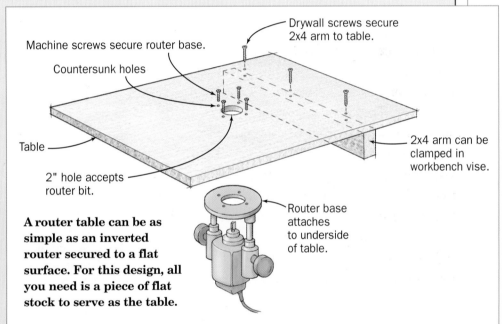

Machine screws secure router base.

Drywall screws secure 2x4 arm to table.

Countersunk holes

Table

2" hole accepts router bit.

2x4 arm can be clamped in workbench vise.

Router base attaches to underside of table.

A router table can be as simple as an inverted router secured to a flat surface. For this design, all you need is a piece of flat stock to serve as the table.

Trimming the case

Although it isn't necessary in terms of functionality, trimming the raw plywood edges with a hardwood trim lends the piece a more finished look.

1. At the tablesaw, cut a ¾"-thick length of stock into five strips about ¼" wide. Be sure you have a zero-clearance insert installed in the tablesaw and use a push paddle so that the loose strips won't kick back toward you as they are cut loose. (See "Skill Builder: Using Safety Devices for the Tablesaw" on pp. 84–85).

2. At the tablesaw, use the miter gauge to cut two lengths of trim to match the length of the sides.

3. With the case laid on its back (across sawhorses or on the floor), apply a bead of glue to the front edges of the sides. Set the trim in place and tape it down. You can use brads to secure it, but it's really not necessary. Lengths of painter's tape every 5" will pull the edging tight and help you align it with the edge of the case until the glue sets, as shown in photo G.

4. Cut lengths of trim to match the width of the shelves, then apply them in the same manner as you did on the sides in step 3. Aim for a fit that is tight between the side trim but doesn't force it out of position.

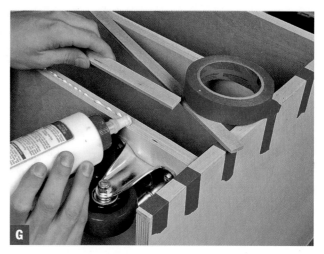

Give it a finished look A thin bead of glue and painter's tape offer plenty of holding power to attach a hardwood edging.

Finishing touches

A few final additions, and you'll be ready to build the top. To attach the top, you'll use glue blocks attached to the base and screwed to the top. You'll also want to drill an access hole to accommodate power cords.

1. Cut lengths of plywood about 2" wide and glue them in place along the top edge. Take care to make sure that they are flush with the top, but not proud of it. Clamp the blocks in place, then use a square to make sure that they are square to the edge of the case, as shown in photo H.

2. Use a 1⅛" or larger drill bit—an inexpensive spade bit will do—to drill a hole at a top corner of the case's back. This will serve as an access hole, allowing you to feed power tools through the case to hide them and keep them safely out of the way.

Add the glue blocks When attaching the glue blocks, make sure they are flush (or slightly below flush) to the top edge the case.

What You'll Need

- **Scrap plywood, at least 10" x 10"**
- **Dado set**

A dado set on your tablesaw enables you to cut grooves, dadoes, and rabbets—joints that work well in case pieces.

A dado set features two circular blades that look just like regular sawblades, as well as a set of diamond-shaped knickers. When you install a dado set, you can use one knicker or multiple knickers to establish the correct thickness. To set up for a dado cut, you install one full blade, add as many knickers as you need to reach the desired width of the cut, then install the other full blade on the opposite side.

From time to time, you'll be unable to reach the desired width by using the knickers alone, but using spacers will allow you to dial in the width of the cut fairly precisely.

Rabbets, Dadoes, and Grooves

Rabbet
Cut along the edge of a board.

Groove
Groove runs with the grain of the wood.

Dado
Dado runs against the grain of the wood.

Once you've mastered these three joints, you'll be able to put together case and drawer assemblies smoothly and square.

You can buy spacers—which look like thin metal washers with a wide diameter—and insert them between the knickers until you reach the desired depth.

Once you've set the dado for the correct width of cut, you're ready to cut dadoes or rabbets. Small benchtop saws usually can't manage much more than a ¼" depth before stalling, but for most case construction, ¼" is plenty.

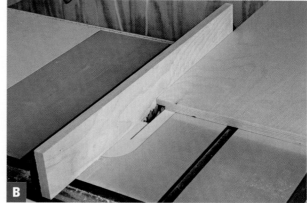

Using a Dado Set with a Rip Fence

1. Remove the regular blade on your saw. Install the dado set and adjust it to the desired width.

2. Raise the blade so that about ¼" protrudes above the table height.

3. Mark the dado or rabbet location on the board, then align your rip fence to guide the cut. If you're cutting a dado, the narrowest portion of the stock should be placed on the fence side of the blade, as shown in photo A. If you're cutting a rabbet, use an auxiliary fence and position it so that it is only a hair shy of the blade, as shown in photo B.

4. Take test passes to see if the width of the dado is correct and to set the depth of cut. You'll want to take the cut a little slower than you would with a single blade, and you may need to apply a little downward pressure to keep the stock from rising off the table.

Using a Dado Set with a Miter Gauge

1. Remove the regular blade on your saw. Install the dado set to the desired width.

2. Use a miter gauge (outfitted with an auxiliary fence) to hold your stock as you pass it over the blade. Be sure to keep a tight hold on the stock, as shown in photo C.

3. Set the depth of the cut, but be sure to limit the depth of the cut to about ¼" at a time.

4. Take test passes to see if the width of the dado is correct.

Building the Top

T he top of a router table is where all the action happens. There are a number of quality commercial tops available, but because making one is straightforward, I've never seen the need to buy one. The top seen here is simply two layers of ¾" MDF that are face-glued to form a top that is 1½" thick. The edges of the MDF are covered with a hardwood trim to keep the edges from getting damaged and to give it a finished look. Sealed with a layer of shellac and coated with a layer of wax, MDF provides a flat, even surface that allows workpieces to slide smoothly. It works beautifully.

Gluing Up the Top

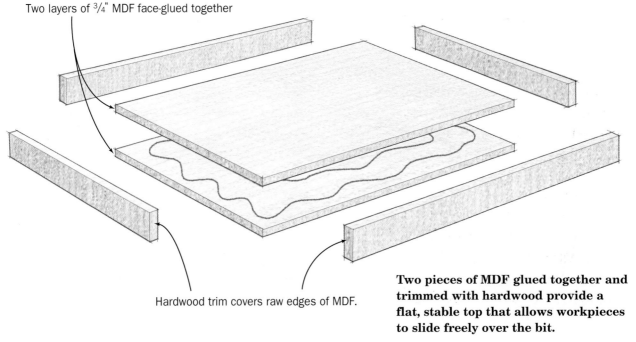

Two layers of ¾" MDF face-glued together

Hardwood trim covers raw edges of MDF.

Two pieces of MDF glued together and trimmed with hardwood provide a flat, stable top that allows workpieces to slide freely over the bit.

Glue up the MDF

1. Start by cutting two pieces of MDF to size at the tablesaw or with a circular saw and guide. Because it's difficult to glue them together with the edges exactly aligned, I prefer to cut them slightly oversize (about ¼" in both length and width) and then recut them after the glue dries.

2. Use a small paint roller to spread a thin, almost transparent layer of glue on the two faces of the MDF. Set them on a flat surface with the two glued faces together. Drive two to four 1¼" screws through the bottom, placing them in the center so they'll be cut out when you remove a section for the insert. Then clamp around the edges of the assembly and let it sit for at least an hour.

3. Once the clamps come off, retrim the top to final size. You can do this with either a circular saw and cutting guide or at the tablesaw.

Trim the top

With the top cut to final size, it's time to install a hardwood trim. I used maple trim around the top of the table shown here because it is similar in color to the Baltic birch used on the base. If you chose a different plywood for the base, choose a matching hardwood to trim the top.

1. Start by ripping the trim to width at the tablesaw. Use two pieces of scrap MDF held on edge to locate the fence, then cut enough trim to cover all four edges of the top.

2. Cut the two side pieces of trim to length. Test-fit them against the top. If they're even slightly long, cut them shorter, because otherwise they'll keep the front and rear trim from sitting flush to the edge.

3. Spread a thin layer of glue on both sides of the top and on the trim. Apply the trim to the top and use painter's tape to hold it in

position until you get all the clamps in place. When clamping down, make sure that the trim is not proud of the face. If it comes out a little high in a few spots, you can trim it flush with a block plane, but it's better to avoid the problem altogether.

4. With the side trim installed, you're ready to glue on the front and back trim. Cut it to the correct length and be sure to test-fit, as shown in photo I. Apply thin layers of glue to the trim and the top, and put them together. Clamp the trim in place and leave the clamps on for about an hour, as shown in photo J.

Trim the top When applying the hardwood trim to the top, set the edge flush to the top face of the MDF.

Clamp it up Tape helps hold the trim in place until the clamps go on.

Make a cutout to accommodate the top

Once the clamps come off, you're ready to install the insert. The router will be secured to the insert and the insert dropped into place in the top. To make room for the insert, cut a rectangular hole through the top so that the router is able to fit through it. You'll then rout a ⅝" ledge to catch the edges of the insert and hold it flush to the top.

1. The first step is to locate the insert on the top. Use a combination square to center it on the top, then trace around the insert with a pencil, as shown in photo K.

Trace around the insert plate With the router insert centered on the top, mark the outline with a pencil.

2. Remove the insert and draw another line inset ⅝" from the outline of the insert, as shown in photo L. The inner line establishes the cutout, while the space between the lines denotes the ledge you'll rout.

3. Drill holes on the inside corners of the inner line you've just drawn and use them as access holes for a jigsaw, as shown in photo M. Make the cutout with a jigsaw, as shown in photo N on p. 106.

Draw the inset line Mark ⅝" inside the first insert outline you made. You'll cut away everything inside these new lines.

Drill access holes for the jigsaw In order to drop the blade of the jigsaw through the top, drill holes inside the corners of the inset lines.

Rout a ledge to hold the router

The next step is to rout a ledge that will allow the insert to sit flush to the top and keep the router from falling through. You'll need a straight bit with a diameter that matches the rounded corners of the insert. The bit also needs to be bearing driven, with the bearing mounted on the shaft end of the cutter. You can buy bits with this arrangement or buy a straight bit and then install separate bearings over the shaft of the bit. You'll also need a cutting length on the cutterhead of no more than ¾" so that you'll be able to guide it against a ¾"-thick template. For the Bench Dog Tools insert I used, I needed a straight bit with a ¾" diameter. If you choose a different insert, check the installation instructions to determine the diameter bit you'll need. To guide the router, you'll need a few scraps of ¾" plywood with straight edges.

Cut out the center Use a jigsaw to follow the inset lines between the access holes. Once complete, the inverted router drops though this cutout.

1. Set the insert in place on the top, aligning the edges with the outline you marked out earlier.

A quick router template With the insert set in place, clamp four straightedge guides that abut the edges of the insert.

2. Grab a few scraps of ¾" plywood and clamp them in place against all four sides of the insert, as shown in photo O. Because you need a relatively tight fit at the corners (within ¼" is fine) to guide the bearing on the router bit, you may have to trim the length of the end guides so that all four pieces will fit on the top at once. Use at least two clamps on each of the guides, and place them so that the base of your handheld router is not impeded.

3. Install a bearing-guided straight bit in a plunge router and tighten it down. Put a scrap of the same stock you used for the template guide and the insert together, hold up the bit to the pieces, and set the depth of the bit to the combined thickness of the scrap piece and the insert, as shown in photo P. Set the depth stop on your router so that it won't allow you to plunge any deeper than this measurement. It's better to set the depth a little shallow than it is to set it too deep. For more on using bearing-guided router bits, see "Using Bearing-Guided Bits" at right.

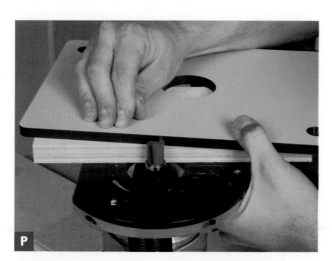

Determine the depth of cut Because the bit's bearing will ride on the guide stock when routing, set the depth of the router bit to match the thickness of the insert plus the thickness of the guide stock. Be sure to engage the depth stop so that you won't cut too deep.

USING BEARING-GUIDED BITS

Bearing-guided router bits feature a free-spinning bearing that rides against a guide or template as you cut. The bearing allows you to follow the exact edge of a pattern or guide by lining it up with the line you're trying to follow.

Bearing-guided bits come in one of two forms—either the bearing is mounted above the bit's cutterhead (on the shaft) or below it. For cutting the insert ledge, you'll want a bearing mounted on the shaft above the cutting edge. This bit will come in handy around the shop for numerous other tasks. In the future, you'll be able to cut templates in various rectilinear or curved designs, mount them to your stock, and cut multiple exact replicas of the template.

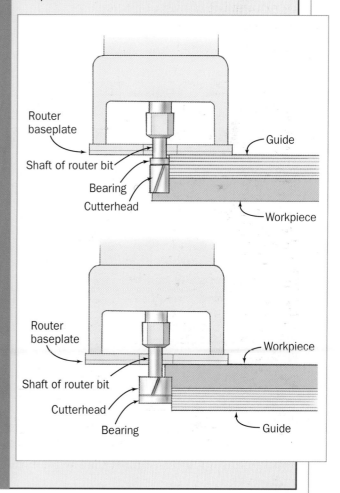

Q

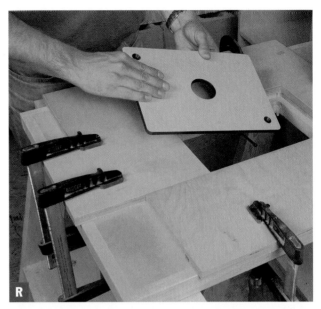

R

Rout the ledge Raise the router so that your first pass is only about ⅛" deep. Then plunge the router bit to full depth and complete the cut. Be sure to rout in a clockwise direction.

Test the fit Before removing the template, set the insert in place. Test the depth against the exposed part of the top at the corners of the template. If necessary, lower the bit and rerout the ledge.

4. To cut the ledge in the top, start by raising the router bit, turning on the router, and slowly plunging into the cut. It's best to begin with a shallow cut—about ⅛" to ¹⁄₁₆"—and proceed around all four sides in a clockwise direction. Making sure your bit stays engaged on the template, lower the bit to full depth and complete the cut, as shown in photo Q.

5. Before you remove the guides, test-fit your insert in the opening, as shown in photo R. A tiny bit of the top will be exposed at the corners, where you can tell you if you're at the correct depth or not. Whatever the result, don't fret. If the ledge is a little too shallow, you can lower the bit and take another pass. If it's too deep, you can shim up the edges of the insert with masking tape.

6. At this point, you should apply a coat of finish to the top. With plywood, I'll often simply wax the surfaces and be done with it, but I prefer to lay a coat of shellac onto MDF. A

S

Rub on a finish Applying shellac is easy and fast. It also seals the faces of the MDF against moisture. Be sure to finish the bottom as well as the top.

light coat applied with a lint-free rag works fine. I use an old, worn-out T-shirt that's had too many runs through the washing machine, as shown in photo S.

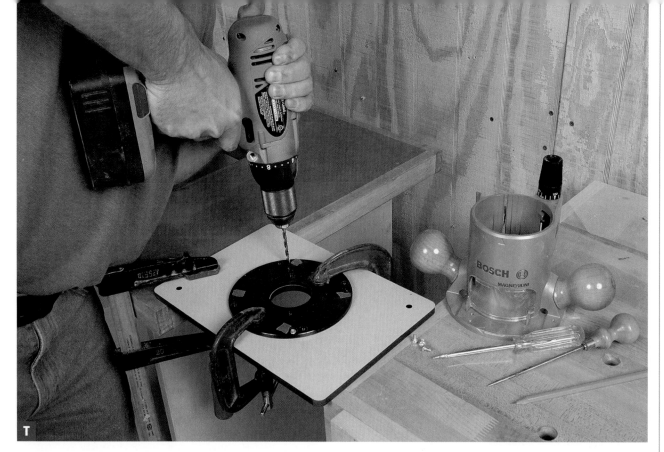

Drill the insert to match the baseplate With the baseplate off your router and centered on the insert, mark and drill holes for attaching the router's base.

Attach the router to the insert and the top to the base

To get the router table up and running, you'll need to attach the router to the insert so that you'll be able to invert the router to expose the bit above the table. Actually, you don't mount the router, only the base. Once the router table is set up, you'll seldom, if ever, remove the base of the router from the insert. To use the router table, just slide the router motor into the base and lock it in place.

1. Locate the router on the insert by setting it in place atop the insert. If your insert has a clearly indicated bottom or top, make sure you set the router on the insert's bottom. Then adjust the router so that, when installed, the power switch and bit-raising adjustments are accessible from the front of the table. Center the router in the opening on the insert and

mark both the router's baseplate and the insert so you can relocate the baseplate once it's removed from the base. Because you can't write on the router's slick baseplate, I mark it using a piece of tape.

2. Remove the router from the base and remove the baseplate from the router. Many baseplates have numerous holes, so be sure to mark those you're actually using with pieces of tape before you remove the screws. You won't actually need the baseplate to use your router table, but it makes a convenient guide for drilling the insert. Set the baseplate in place on the insert and double-check to make sure it's centered on the bit opening in the insert. Once you're happy with the position, clamp it in place. Mark the centers of the holes with an awl or the end of a nail.

5. Once the insert is drilled, screw the base directly to the insert (you won't need the baseplate for using the router in a table). To ensure that the base is centered and pulled tight, install all four screws before you tighten any of them down. With the base installed, slide the router into the base, lock it down, and then set the whole assembly in the router table, as shown in photo V.

6. To attach the top to the glue blocks on the base, drill through the glue blocks and into the top from underneath. Predrill the screw holes so that you won't split the glue blocks. You only need to sink about two 1½" drywall screws through each block. Because the screws won't be seen, there's no reason to countersink them. Now, you're ready to rout.

Countersink for the screw heads So that the heads of the screws won't interfere with work on the table, use a countersink bit to recess the heads.

3. Choose a drill bit just a hair larger in diameter than your screws (it's best to test the fit on a scrap of wood first). Then drill through the baseplate into the insert, using the baseplate as a guide, as shown in photo T on p. 109.

4. With the screw holes drilled, remove the baseplate, flip over the insert, and countersink the holes so that the attachment screws will be buried beneath the insert, as shown in photo U. Take care not to go too deep—aim for just enough to bury the screw heads.

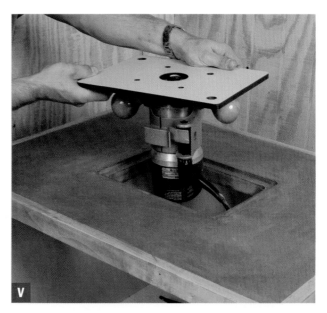

Install the insert Once the base is attached, lock the router into place and then drop the whole assembly into the top of the router table.

outer fences can be as elaborate as you'd like them to be. They can, however, be as simple as grabbing a piece of loose stock from around the shop and clamping it in place on the top of the router. Make sure the fence stock—which can be either plywood or hardwood—has a straight edge. And if you're in a situation where you need to bury a portion of the fence in the router—like rabbeting or profiling an edge—cut a notch in the fence stock to surround the bit. A handsaw or tablesaw makes cutting the notch quick work.

Building the Fence

Most of the work done with a router table involves registering your work against a fence and passing it over the rotating bit. There are almost as many different fence designs as there are people who have router tables. A fence can be as simple as a piece of loose stock clamped to the table (see "A Quick Fence" above) or as elaborate as you are willing to make it.

A Dedicated Router Fence

Made from ¾" plywood and joined with biscuits, this router fence is easily made, but it works as well as most commercial versions.

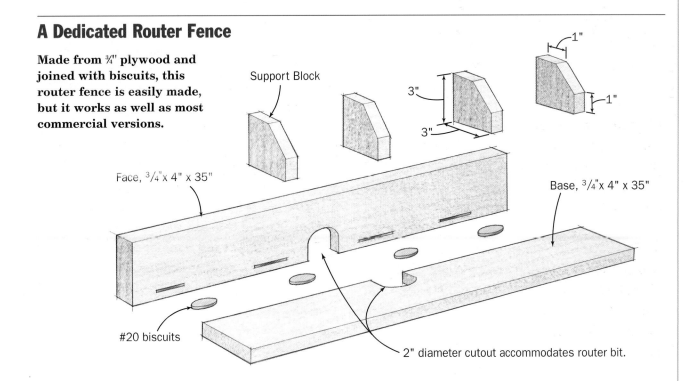

Support Block

3"

3"

3"

1"

1"

Face, ³/₄"x 4" x 35"

Base, ³/₄"x 4" x 35"

#20 biscuits

2" diameter cutout accommodates router bit.

I suggest building a basic, right-angle fence that allows you to attach different auxiliary fences in place to accommodate bits of varying sizes and profiles. Building this fence is a quick task, but it's really all you need to put your router table to work. I clamp it in

place with whatever small clamps are around the shop, but you can add a clamping system that is permanent. You can also add a dust-collection chute that collects dust through the fence.

Building the fence takes only a few scraps of plywood or MDF. I put it together with biscuits, but drywall screws would work as well. One word of caution: If you use screws to join the fence, make sure you place them far enough from the center of the fence so that there's no risk of a spinning bit hitting one.

Cut the parts to size

1. Begin by cutting all the parts to size at the tablesaw.

2. The support blocks for the fence can be cut into small squares at the tablesaw, then the angled corners can be trimmed with either a handsaw or jigsaw.

3. Locate the center of the fence and make round cutouts to accommodate the bit. You can use a compass and draw out a radius of about two inches, but it's often easiest to grab whatever round item you have in the shop and trace it, as shown in photo A.

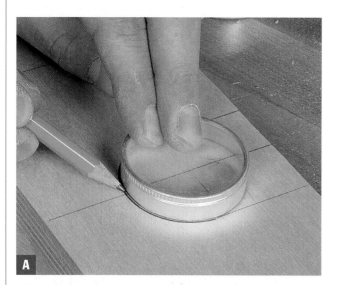

Round templates abound You can use a compass to dial in a two inch opening in the fence, but the exact size is not critical. I just grab whatever round canister is on hand and trace around its perimeter.

Cut the fence opening Use a jigsaw to make cutouts in both the face and base of the fence.

Biscuit the fence Mark and cut mating biscuit slots on the base of the fence.

The fence comes together Once the parts are biscuited and the openings are cut, you're ready to join the base to the face. Attach the braces to make sure it stays square.

You're ready to rout To put the fence to use, just clamp it in place on the top of the router table.

4. Once you draw the outline, make the cuts on the face and base using a jigsaw with a narrow blade, as shown in photo B.

5. Mark centerlines for biscuit slots on both the base and the fence. Use a biscuit joiner to make the biscuit slots. To make the biscuit slots on the base, hold the workpiece flat on the benchtop and plunge in the biscuit joiner. To biscuit the fence, hold it at a right angle against a benchstop or other secure right angle, then plunge in the biscuit joiner, as shown in photo C.

6. Add glue to the slots and slide the biscuits in place, as shown in photo D. Clamp the face and base together. Glue and clamp the support blocks into place.

7. To put the fence to work, simply clamp it down to the top of the router table, as shown in photo E. To make small adjustments, clamp one end down and swing the other into place, then clamp it down. Using practice pieces is a good way to help you align cuts.

Whether at the tablesaw or router, you'll run into situations where using your normal fence just won't cut it. Both the tablesaw and router table projects in this book offer easy solutions for attaching auxiliary fences.

On the Tablesaw

Attaching an auxiliary fence to your tablesaw's stock fence is safer than using the metal fence that comes with your saw because accidental dings won't harm the cutting edges of your blade. When it comes time to rabbet stock, an auxiliary fence allows you to bury part of the blade in the fence. Most fences are equipped with holes that allow you to bolt an auxiliary fence directly to it. A length of plywood and a few screws are all that's needed. To keep stock moving smoothly across the fence, give it a good coating of wax from time to time.

MITER-GAUGE FENCE Miter gauges come in handy around the tablesaw, but their small face makes it difficult to keep long stock aligned. Attaching an auxiliary fence to your miter gauge provides better support to the stock you're cross-

Using a miter gauge A longer miter fence provides better support as you crosscut.

cutting, allowing you to crosscut longer stock safely and accurately. Attach an auxiliary fence that is long enough to cover the blade completely, and cut right through it when you cut. The extra length adds stability and prevents tearout where the blade exits the workpiece. Most miter gauges come with access holes for attaching an auxiliary fence.

Using a high fence To cut along the edge of a wide board—for grooving or profiling an edge—use a high fence and clamp a featherboard in place above the blade.

HIGH FENCE At some point in a future project, you're going to want to bevel or dado the edge of a panel, and to do so you'll need a high fence—but you really don't need anything but a flat piece of plywood screwed into place. A high fence can be attached directly to the subfence. Whenever you cut a tall panel against a high fence, be sure to use a featherboard to keep your stock from getting away from you.

On the Router Table

As with the tablesaw, there are many options for router-table auxiliary fences and safety devices, and the concepts are the same. If you're profiling an edge with work flat on the router table, you might want to attach a zero-clearance fence to prevent tearout. If you're grooving the edge of a tall board and need to hold the work horizontally, you'll want to attach a higher fence. The fence design shown below makes attaching any auxiliary fence quite simple; just screw it in place through the upright face of the fence. And remember, if

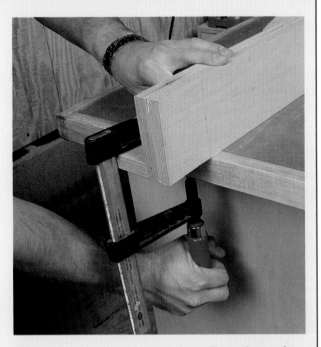

Zero-clearance fences work best For a fence that matches the profile of the bit, clamp down one end of the fence, then slowly push the other end toward the bit. Keep a good hold of the fence and cut only a little at a time.

Attach a sub-fence If you drill through the face of the fence, you'll be able to screw on an array of sub-fences with little fuss.

the task at hand would otherwise entail passing your hands within 6" of the rotating bit, clamp featherboards in place on the fence or tabletop, as you would on a tablesaw.

ZERO-CLEARANCE INSERT To make an auxiliary fence a zero-clearance, either cut out the profile on the tablesaw or on the router table itself. To do it on the router table, clamp down one end of the fence and leave the other loose. With the fence clear of the bit, power up the router. Then, slowly, pivot the loose end of the fence toward the bit. Allow the bit to engage the fence only slightly, then back off. Then swing it toward the bit again, slowly. Repeat this process until the fence is cut out just a little deeper than you need for cutting stock. Then set the fence to the correct location, and you're ready for work.

Building the Drawers

The drawers for this router table are built using very traditional methods, and the same methods will work for everything from side tables to sideboards to chests-of-drawers. They aren't hardwood high-style dovetailed drawers, but the idea is otherwise the same. The drawer front is cut from ¾" plywood, the sides and back from ½", and the bottom from ¼". The front is attached to the sides with a simple rabbet joint, and the back is set into two dadoes cut into the sides. The bottom slides into a groove on the bottom of the sides and front.

Building this drawer also teaches the basics of using a router table. All the joinery can be cut on a tablesaw outfitted with a dado set, but you've just built a router table, so why not use it? The instructions below are for building a single drawer, but you'll want to make doubles of all the parts to construct two matching drawers to fill out the bottom of the case. Once the drawers are built, use them to store all the wrenches, collets, and router parts that are hard to keep track of. I also make bit storage blocks, so I can easily find whatever bit I need.

Drawer Construction

Building this drawer design teaches all the basic elements of a traditional drawer. Pegged joints give it a bit of style.

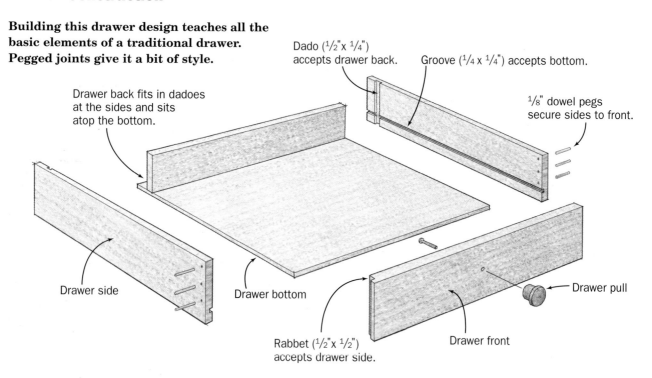

Dado (½" x ¼") accepts drawer back.

Groove (¼ x ¼") accepts bottom.

Drawer back fits in dadoes at the sides and sits atop the bottom.

⅛" dowel pegs secure sides to front.

Drawer side

Drawer bottom

Rabbet (½" x ½") accepts drawer side.

Drawer front

Drawer pull

Cut the parts to size

1. To make a template, hold a piece of stock up to the drawer opening and mark the height, then cut it to size on the tablesaw. Test the fit by sliding the stock into the drawer opening. Leave about ¹⁄₁₆" slop so that the fit isn't too tight. Then cut the sides, back, and front to the same height on the tablesaw. (You should be able to use the same height for both drawers, but check your template in both openings before you cut anything. If there's a discrepancy, just cut parts for the two drawers separately, using the correct measures. If measurements are the same, you can cut the parts for both drawers at the same time.)

2. Hold the front up to the base to measure and mark for width. Leave about 1/16" of room around the front so that the fit isn't too tight. Cut the front to width using a miter gauge on your tablesaw, taking care not to trim it too short. Test the fit. If it's too long, trim off a little more. Once you're happy with the fit, mark and cut the drawer back to the same length.

3. Slide the sides into the drawer opening and mark them for length. Remember to leave them 1/4" shy of full depth to allow for the depth of the rabbet on the drawer front. Cut the drawer sides to length.

Cut the joinery

1. The drawer front is rabbeted on both ends to accept the drawer sides. Install a 1/2" straight bit into the router table and raise it so that 1/2" of the cutter is exposed above the table surface. To set the depth, hold the drawer side against the fence and adjust the clamps until the exposed portion of the bit matches the width of the drawer side.

2. To make rabbeting cuts on the drawer stock, you'll need to use a backer board—a piece of square stock (roughly 10" x 10" square) to guide the cut. Hold the backer board against the fence and then butt the drawer front against the backer board and the end against the fence. Flip on the power, then pass the stock over the fence in a slow, smooth motion, as shown in photo F.

Rabbet the drawer front **Butt the drawer front against a square backer board, then keep both the backer board and the drawer front against the fence throughout the cut.**

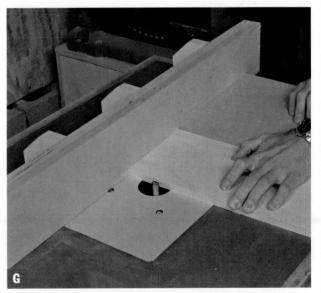

Dado the sides **The back of the drawer sits in dadoes near the backs of the drawer sides. Use a backer board to keep the cut square to the edge while routing the dadoes.**

Routers, like any tool with a cutting edge and a power switch, can be dangerous. The key to working safely at the router table is to respect the tool.

- Always pass work from the right side of the fence to the left. Position yourself on the front right corner of the table and make sure both feet are firmly planted.

- Never rout freehand at the router table. Work should always be registered against a fence or starting pin. Keep the stock flat to the fence.

- Never rout against a fence unless it is clamped firmly in place.

- Pass the work over the bit at a slow, even feed rate. If you go too slowly, the cutter will start to burn the stock. Too fast, and the router will make a loud, whining noise. With practice, you'll hear the difference.

- Keep your fingers at least 6" from the spinning bit at all times. Use featherboards, push paddles, and push sticks when necessary.

- Routers produce lots of noise. Wear earplugs or earmuffs.

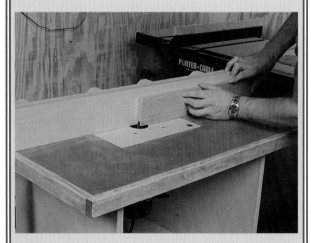

Find a comfortable stance **Stand to the right side of the router bit and make sure the floor is clear so you can move toward the left as you rout.**

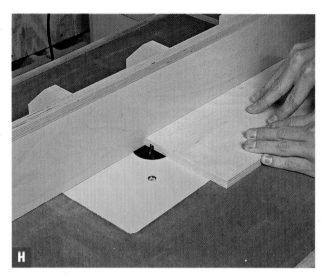

Groove for the bottom **The bottom of the drawer sits in a groove on the front and sides. Use a backer board.**

3. To dado the sides to accept the back, lower the bit to make a cut about ¼" deep, then repeat the cutting process you used to rabbet the drawer front in step 2, as shown in photo G on p. 117.

4. The front and the sides are grooved to accept the drawer bottom. Use a ¼" straight bit, set it to make a ¼"-deep cut, and offset the fence about ⅜" (so that you're cutting a groove that starts ⅜" up from the bottom of the drawer). Cut the grooves, as shown in photo H.

5. Once the grooves are cut, use the tablesaw to trim the drawer back to its final height. Remember, it sits on top of the bottom, so the height will equal the height of the side minus the height of the groove. Set up the tablesaw using a grooved side to locate the fence, then make the cut. Once it's dry-fitted, trim the back to a length that fits tightly in the dadoes.

Install the bottom and assemble the drawer

1. To dry-fit all the parts, you'll first need to cut the drawer bottom to size. To gauge its width, measure the distance between the rabbets on the drawer front, then add ½" to account for the grooves in the drawer sides.

2. The length of the bottom is not as finicky because the back sits directly on the bottom. Just measure from inside the drawer front to the back of the drawer back and add ¼" to accommodate the groove on the front. Then make the cut on your tablesaw. Dry-fit all the parts and test their fit in the drawer opening.

3. Once the drawer parts have been dry-fitted and all the joints close up, you're ready for glue-up. Apply glue and either nails or dowel pegs to join the drawer front to the sides (see "Skill Builder: Pegging Joints" on pp. 120–121). Then apply a bead of glue to the ends of the drawer back and slide it into place, as shown in photo I. The bottom slides into place on

Install the bottom The bottom slides into place in the grooves on the drawer sides and front.

the grooves, but there's no need to glue it in, as shown in photo J.

4. Add either nails or dowels to hold the back in place, then use a nail or screw to secure the bottom to the back of the drawer, as shown in photo K. With that done, you're ready to slide the drawer into the opening and attach whatever drawer pulls you prefer.

Slide the back in place With the front pegged and clamped together, glue the back into place on the dadoes on the sides. You can nail or peg the joint for reinforcement.

A screw secures the bottom There's no need to glue the bottom into place. A single screw driven through the bottom into the drawer back holds it in place.

What You'll Need

- ⅛" drill bit
- ⅛" dowel
- Small handsaw or backsaw
- Small (8 oz. to 13 oz.) hammer
- Combination square
- Drill/driver
- Chisel, at least 1" wide, or sandpaper

The pegged joint is a standard in traditional furniture. Historically, it's been used to pin through a mortise and into a tenon, but it can also be used in place of nails on basic joinery like dadoes and rabbets. Not only do the pins lend strength to the joint, but they also add a decorative touch. You can use a plain dowel in the same or a contrasting wood. I usually opt for a contrasting wood, because I like the look a little better. When you're building a piece of furniture for your home, pegged joints lend a more refined look.

The joints on both the front rabbet and the rear dado on the drawer of this router table can be pegged.

1. Start by applying a layer of glue to the joint, then clamp it up. Make sure the corners are square with a tri- or combination square. You can either let the glue dry completely and then move on to step 2 or keep the clamps in place throughout the pegging process and move on right away.

2. Use a combination square to mark out three equally spaced points on the side of the joint, then drill the holes using a ⅛" drill bit, as shown in photo A. Make sure to drill at least 1" into the drawer front.

3. Once the holes are drilled, you're ready for the pegs. To make the pegs, cut the dowel into lengths of approximately 1½", using a

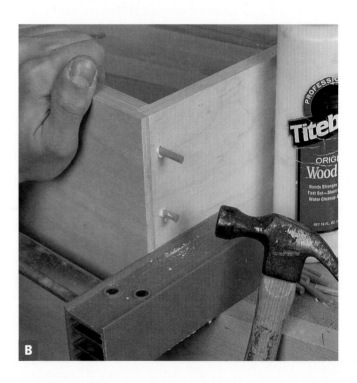

C

handsaw. Put a little glue on the ends of the pegs, then use a hammer to tap them into the holes you drilled in step 2, as shown in photo B. You'll know when you've hit the full depth of the hole because you'll hear a difference in tone as you tap on the peg.

4. Now the dowels are in place, and you're ready to trim them flush to the side of the drawer. Start by sawing them off with a small handsaw or backsaw. Hold the side of the saw flush to the drawer side, as shown in photo C, and you'll be pretty close to flush.

5. Trim and smooth the end of the sawn peg with a sharp chisel. Lay the flat side of the chisel against the side of the drawer and carefully trim the pegs flush. Or, if you'd rather, you can trim the pegs with sandpaper—just take care not to round the edge of the drawer front.

INSTALLING A POWER SWITCH

To me, shutting off the power has always seemed like the most dangerous part of using a router table. Normally, you make a cut and then reach under the router table to turn off the router at its source. But until it's switched off, the bit spins, ready to catch any stray part that finds its way onto the table. And to turn off the router, you have to reach up into the dark, hard-to-see portion of the table, close to where the bit is spinning.

The solution is to install a power switch so that you can turn the router on and off without reaching under the table. If you're more savvy with electrical work than I am, you can wire your own power box, plug the router into it, and then install a switch. But installing a prewired power box like the one seen here (from Bench Dog Tools) is easier. The switch turns off easily when the work is done, but it also has a safety switch that keeps the machine from turning on accidentally.

Installing the switch couldn't be easier. Simply screw it in place under the top or on the side of your base. Then plug the router into the switch and plug the switch into a wall outlet. Cords can be looped through the access hole in the back of the base to keep them out of your way as you work.

Storage

Everyone loves buying tools, and many even enjoy the sometimes finicky work of tuning them up. But with all those tools comes the need for tool storage that is safe and out of the way. A shop without a logical storage system is just a big pile of lumber and metal—not the kind of place where you can expect to get much work done.

In this chapter, you'll build a number of different projects that provide plenty of storage for the basic workshop: banks of drawers, cabinets with doors, lumber and clamp racks, and a smart pegboard system that keeps your most-used tools close at hand.

All of these projects are sized to fit a small shop, where space is at a premium. But the overall sizes of these projects are not critical. If you need larger storage cabinets, a full wall of pegboard panels, or only enough lumber storage to handle a single project at a time, adjust the sizes of the projects to fit your space and needs.

Many woodworkers feel that they should be building furniture or trimming the windows in their house instead of building storage units for their shop. While it's true that you can buy similar storage units at home centers, building your own storage units allows you to design the units to fit your needs exactly. It's also a good way to learn the skills that will improve your woodworking for building more critical pieces.

What You'll Learn

- Building no-fuss drawers
- Cutting dadoes with a router
- Making drawer pulls without hardware
- Installing a face frame
- Adding adjustable shelves
- Using butt hinges to hang doors
- Cutting mortises by hand
- Anchoring projects to wall studs
- Using a cleat system for hanging projects

A drawer for every need **Quick-to-make shop drawers offer lots of storage.**

The projects in this chapter are more than quick fixes for getting lumber off the floor and tools off the workbench. They're also designed to teach skills that are valuable to any woodworker. And wouldn't you rather learn how to build a chest of drawers using plywood than risk mistakes on expensive cherry or the irreplaceable walnut boards that came from a tree on your grandparents' farm?

The router table and tablesaw workstation projects in earlier chapters showed a couple of different methods for building drawers. And while those same methods work just fine for storage drawers, the ones built here are an even simpler design. What's more, you don't need hardware; a drilled hole is a serviceable drawer pull and an interesting design element as well. You can use this same drawer design to outfit cases of all sizes and shapes.

Building the two-door cabinet is a crash course in cabinet and furniture making. When you learn to build a cabinet, you learn how to build a simple bookcase, add adjustable shelves, and apply a face frame. When it's

time to hang the doors, you'll learn methods that work on everything from your home's front door to the doors in your bathroom vanity. You'll learn a clever method for hanging cabinets—or anything—on the wall.

You'll also learn how to build the small projects necessary to keep any shop from being cluttered—racks for storing lumber and clamps and customized tool boards to help keep everything organized.

Throughout the process of building these projects, you'll pick up ideas for building other storage systems and also learn a number of methods that will improve your woodworking skills. Not to mention, it's a good way to clean up your shop.

Case of Drawers

Case Construction

Though designed to fit below the workbench built earlier in this book, the case of drawers shown here can be adapted to fit numerous uses around the shop or home.

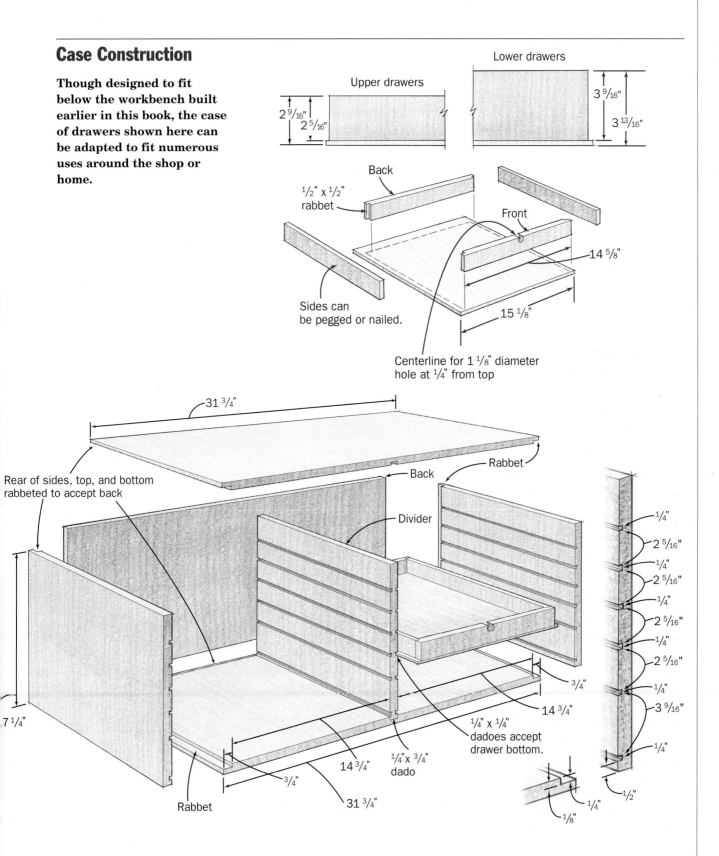

Upper drawers

$2^{9}/_{16}$"
$2^{5}/_{16}$"

Lower drawers

$3^{9}/_{16}$"
$3^{13}/_{16}$"

Back

$^{1}/_{2}$" x $^{1}/_{2}$" rabbet

Front

Sides can be pegged or nailed.

$14^{5}/_{8}$"

$15^{1}/_{8}$"

Centerline for $1^{1}/_{8}$" diameter hole at $^{1}/_{4}$" from top

$31^{3}/_{4}$"

Rear of sides, top, and bottom rabbeted to accept back

Back

Rabbet

Divider

$^{1}/_{4}$"
$2^{5}/_{16}$"
$^{1}/_{4}$"
$2^{5}/_{16}$"
$^{1}/_{4}$"
$2^{5}/_{16}$"
$^{1}/_{4}$"
$2^{5}/_{16}$"
$^{1}/_{4}$"
$3^{9}/_{16}$"
$^{1}/_{4}$"

$7^{1}/_{4}$"

Rabbet

$^{3}/_{4}$"

$14^{3}/_{4}$"

$^{1}/_{4}$" x $^{3}/_{4}$" dado

$31^{3}/_{4}$"

$^{1}/_{4}$" x $^{1}/_{4}$" dadoes accept drawer bottom.

$14^{3}/_{4}$"

$^{3}/_{4}$"

$^{1}/_{8}$"
$^{1}/_{4}$"
$^{1}/_{2}$"

Quantity	Part	Actual Size	What to Buy
2	Case sides	¾" x 19¼" x 17⅜"	One sheet of ¾" plywood is enough for all case parts.
1	Case top	¾" x 19¼" x 31¾"	
1	Case bottom	¾" x 19¼" x 31¾"	
1	Divider	¾" x 18½" x 17⅜"	
1	Case back	¼" x 17⅜" x 30¼"	Two sheets of ¼" plywood are enough for the back and the drawer bottoms.
10	Upper drawer fronts	⅝" x 2⁵⁄₁₆" x 14⅝"	½" or ¾" also works for the drawer fronts and backs.
10	Upper drawer backs	⅝" x 2⁵⁄₁₆" x 14⅝"	
20	Upper drawer sides	½ x 2⁵⁄₁₆" x 17½"	
2	Lower drawer fronts	⅝" x 3⁹⁄₁₆" x 17½"	You can substitute ½" plywood for the drawer fronts and backs.
2	Lower drawer backs	⅝" x 3⁹⁄₁₆" x 17½"	
4	Lower drawer sides	½" x 3⁹⁄₁₆" x 17½"	
12	Drawer bottoms	¼" x 15⅛" x 18½"	
1 box	Finish nails	1¼"	You'll only need a few, but it's best to buy a box so you'll have them on hand.
1 box	Brads	1"	
3	Drywall screws	1½" long	
	Misc.		Yellow glue, natural-colored putty (optional), wax, sandpaper, finish (if desired)

Buying Materials

One perk of using this method for drawer making is that no hardware is needed. For this project, I used three different thicknesses of plywood—¾", ½", and ¼". But the plywood thickness is not important for the box back or the drawer sides and fronts, so you can use whatever scrap you have on hand. For the drawers, hardwood scraps work as well as plywood.

- Combination square
- Tape measure or folding rule
- tablesaw with wooden auxiliary fence
- Dado set
- Drill
- 1⅛" Forstner or brad-point bit
- Hammer
- Nail set
- Circular saw and straightedge guide
- Smaller block plane

Adding a bank of drawers to the lower section of a workbench not only gives you much more storage space, but it also adds weight to your bench, making it less likely to shift as you work. You'll find that the height of the drawers is perfect for shop storage, where most of your tools don't need a deep drawer. Chisels, screwdrivers, and some handplanes fit nicely into the shallow upper drawers, and drills and larger handplanes can be stored in the deeper lower drawers.

But this drawer unit can be used in a number of different situations. Adjust the size to accommodate whatever space you have, but use the same straightforward methods to build the drawers. They're great in the shop, but at my house, we've got similar chests of drawers that we use in our laundry room and office.

Small space, lots of storage This drawer unit provides a dozen drawers and plenty of storage for small hand tools and supplies.

Building the Box

The carcase of this drawer unit is sized to fit below the workbench built earlier in the book (see pp. 28–55), but you should adjust the overall measurements to fit your workbench—or any other spot where you could use a case of drawers. You could use a number of different methods to assemble the basic case that houses the drawers, but here we'll assemble the box using rabbets and dadoes. On large case-pieces, it makes the pieces easier to position and hold in place as they go together. You can also use biscuits or simply screw the case together.

Cut the parts to size

All the parts can be cut to size using your tablesaw, but if you don't have large outfeed tables, it may be easier to cut them to rough size first using your circular saw and a cutting guide (see "A Shopmade Cutting Guide" on p. 19).

1. When you measure for the height of the case, leave at least ¼" between the top of the drawer case and the bottom of the aprons on the workbench. You could aim for a tighter fit, but I find it safer to leave a little wiggle room in case either the case or the workbench is slightly out of square.

2. Most tablesaws aren't large enough to cut the top, bottom, and back to length, so use a circular saw and a cutting guide if necessary.

3. The sides, divider, and back can all be cut to the same height using your tablesaw.

Cut the joinery

All the joinery for this project is dadoes and rabbets. If you've got a dado set for your tablesaw, you can cut them easily, but you can also make the cuts using a hand-held plunge router, a straightedge cutting guide, and straight bits. You'll need both ¼" and ¾" straight bits if you use a router. For more on this method, see "Skill Builder: Routing Dadoes and Rabbets" on pp. 130–131. Here, we'll use the dado set on the tablesaw.

1. At your tablesaw, install the dado set and set it up to make a cut ¾" wide and ¼" deep. Install a wooden auxiliary fence on your tablesaw so that the blade won't nick the metal fence as you cut the rabbets. Then butt the auxiliary fence as close as you can to the blade without touching it.

2. To cut the rabbets on the ends of the top and bottom, butt the stock against the fence and pass the ends of the stock over the blade, as shown in photo A. While you have this setup in place, cut rabbets on the rear inside faces of the top, bottom, and two sides to accommodate the back.

3. On the inside faces of the top and the bottom, mark a ¾"-wide dado down the center from the front to the back to accommodate the divider. Adjust the fence to make this cut and guide the top over the dado set, as shown in photo B. Use the same setup to cut the bottom's dado.

4. Cut the top, bottom, sides, and divider to the same depth using your tablesaw. After making the cuts, adjust the fence and trim the depth of the divider another ¾" to allow room for the back.

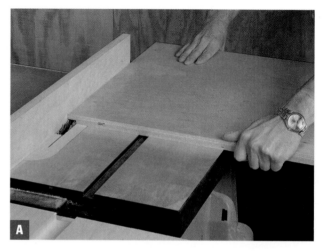

A

Rabbet the top and bottom To rabbet the edges of the top and bottom, install a dado head set to ¾" and run the auxiliary tablesaw fence almost flush to the blade.

B

Dado for the divider Shift the fence and set it to cut a dado down the center of both the top and the bottom.

C

Dado using a single blade **Instead of using a dado set to make the ¼"-wide dado, you can simply make two passes with a single blade**

Cut grooves to accept the drawers

The drawers in this case are not traditional drawers, but they work just as well and are a little less fussy to make. Instead of installing drawer runners in the case, you extend the ends of the drawer bottoms to allow them to ride in grooves cut into the sides of the case. It takes only about 10 minutes at the tablesaw to cut all the grooves, or "runners," for the drawers. You can set up the dado set to cut a groove ¼" wide and ¼" deep, but I find it quicker to make every dado by taking two passes with a single blade.

1. When you lay out the dado locations on the sides and divider, don't forget that ¼" of the top and bottom will be buried in rabbets. It might help to put a mark ¼" down from the top to use as a reference point for measuring. Starting at the ¼" mark on one side piece, measure down another 2⁵⁄₁₆" and mark out a ¼" groove. At the bottom of the groove, meas-

ure another 2⁵⁄₁₆" down and mark out another ¼" groove. Do this all the way down the case (see the bottom drawing on p. 125). The height of the bottom drawer is not critical, so if it winds up a little larger or smaller than the size shown in the drawing, don't worry. (The bottom drawer in this project is 3⁹⁄₁₆".)

2. Set the fence on your tablesaw to the marks for the first groove, then make the cut. Before you adjust the fence for the other cuts, cut the other side piece, as well as both faces of the divider. This way you won't have to measure the cuts on those pieces or reset the saw for those measurements later. If you're using a single blade, edge the fence over and make another pass to cut a groove that is ¼" wide, as shown in photo C. Using the single blade is often quicker than making all the test cuts with the dado set. Once you've made the cut, test the fit with a scrap of ¼" plywood to make sure that the plywood can move smoothly in the groove.

What You'll Need

- **Plunge router**
- **Straight bit**
- **¾"-thick scrap lumber at least 12" x 12"**
- **Scrap of plywood to serve as a straightedge guide**
- **Combination square**

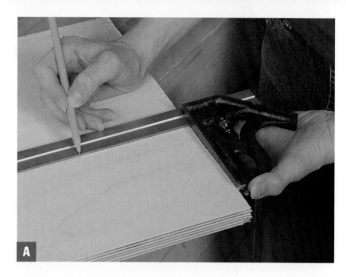

A

Cutting dadoes or rabbets is among the most common tasks performed by a plunge router. I know woodworkers who dedicate a certain router to that task alone, leaving it set up with a ¾" straight bit all the time. A router is a good choice for cutting dadoes and rabbets—it can be less hassle than setting up a dado set on the tablesaw for an exact cut.

To cut dadoes, rabbets, or grooves with a router, you need only a straight bit, sized to the desired width of the cut, and a straightedge guide. (I find a scrap of plywood to be the best choice for a guide.) But before you cut actual workpieces, it's good to practice the task on some scrap stock. The process described below is for cutting dadoes, but the same method works for cutting rabbets on the edge of a board or for cutting grooves.

1. Use a combination square to lay out the edge of the dado on the stock you're cutting, as shown in photo A. Make sure you mark both ends of the dado, so you'll have a reference for both ends of your straightedge guide.

2. With the router unplugged, install the straight bit into the router using the wrenches that came with your machine. Release the plunge lock, push down on the

router, and lock the bit in place with ¼" of the bit exposed below the baseplate.

3. Clamp your workpiece to the bench. With the exposed bit hanging off the edge of the stock, align the bit with the marks for the dado, then butt the straightedge guide against the router to determine its location. Clamp the straightedge to the workpiece at that end. Then move to the other end of the workpiece, align the bit again, and set up and clamp that end of the straightedge, as shown in photo B.

B

4. Once both ends of the guide are clamped down, double-check the setup by measuring the distance between the dado marks and the edge of the guide at both ends. The two measurements should be the same. If they're not, you need to make an adjustment on one end or the other.

5. With the guide clamped securely in place, check the cutting depth of the straight bit and lock the plunge mechanism so that you can't plunge below the desired depth.

6. If your cutting depth is ¼" or less, you can make the cut in a single pass. Otherwise, you'll need to make several passes. Set the router on the workpiece against the guide, with the bit hanging over the left edge of the workpiece. Find a steady stance, get a good grip, then turn on the router and rout slowly from left to right, as shown in photo C.

Assemble the case

1. Before assembling the case, dry-fit all the parts to ensure that everything goes together smoothly and square. Then disassemble.

2. Set the bottom of the case flat on the workbench or another flat surface. Put a thin bead of glue in the dado and the rabbets, then set the sides and divider in place.

3. Put a bead of glue along the top of the divider and the sides, then set the top in place, as shown in photo D.

4. You can apply clamps to hold the assembly together until the glue dries, but assembly will go faster if you secure the top and bottom in place using 1¼" finish nails. Drive nails in place at the front and back of the top along the edges and on the divider, then use a straightedge to locate nails along the centers

Assemble the case **Add a bead of glue on the tops of the sides and the divider, and then add the top.**

of the sides and dividers, as shown in photo E. Use a nail set to bury the nails about ⅛" below the surface. If you'd like, you can use a natural-colored putty to fill the nail holes.

5. Once the top is nailed in place, flip the assembly over. Nail through the bottom into the sides and divider.

6. Flip the base over so that the front is face down. Set the back in place in the rabbets at the back of the case. Use a few finishing nails to secure it in place.

7. Stand the case upright. Measure the diagonals across the corners of the front to make sure the case is square. If the diagonal measurements aren't exactly the same, add a clamp across the long side and tighten until you get the correct measurements.

Why make things difficult? You can clamp the assembly together and wait for the glue to dry, or you can simply drive a few 1½" finish nails into place. For a clean look, use a nail set to bury the nails below the surface.

Building the Drawers

As far as drawers go, this construction method is among the most straightforward. The bottom of the drawer fits into the grooves on the sides and the divider. The drawer box is simply a rabbeted assembly that is nailed together. If you'd like a more refined look, you can use pegs instead of nails to assemble the drawers (for more on this process, see "Skill Builder: Pegging Joints" on pp. 120-121).

1. To make the drawer bottoms, measure and mark the width of the bottoms against the case. Leave about ¹⁄₁₆" on each side to allow the bottom to slide smoothly. If you leave more than that, the drawer might fall out of the grooves. On the tablesaw, cut the drawer bottoms to width.

2. Cut the drawer bottoms to the correct depth. Test the fit to make sure the bottoms line up flush to the front of the case when they're installed, as shown in photo F.

3. To make the drawer fronts, measure and mark the width of the fronts against the case. You want the fronts to be about ⅛" narrower than the opening on the case so that there's a little leeway on both sides of the drawer. Cut the drawer fronts to width on the tablesaw.

4. Measure and mark the depth of the sides against the case. You want the sides to be about 1" shy of the full depth of the case. On the tablesaw, cut the drawer sides to the correct depth.

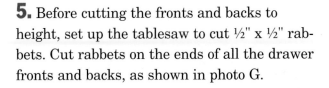

These drawers start at the bottom Cut the drawer bottoms first, aiming for a flush fit at the front of the case.

Cut many rabbets at once Rabbet along the edges of the fronts and backs to accept the drawer sides.

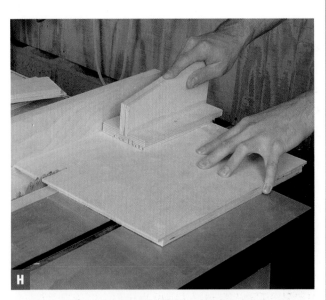

Cut the drawer fronts Once the rabbets have been cut, cut all the drawer fronts to the correct height. Use this same setting to cut all the drawer sides. You'll need to adjust the settings for the lower drawers, which are a different height.

5. Before cutting the fronts and backs to height, set up the tablesaw to cut ½" x ½" rabbets. Cut rabbets on the ends of all the drawer fronts and backs, as shown in photo G.

6. Hold the drawer fronts up to the front of the case and mark the height of each drawer. Remember that your lower drawers are a different height than the upper drawers, so you

should measure and mark each one separately. Cut all the drawer fronts and backs to height, as shown in photo H.

7. After cutting the fronts and backs of the drawers, cut the drawer sides to the same height. You'll need to cut two sides for each drawer, making sure that the height matches the drawer fronts.

Drill for pulls and build the drawers

You can go to any hardware store and buy hardwood or metal pulls that work well for these drawers, but I prefer the look of the drilled pulls used on this design. Also, this way, if you're installing the drawer box under your workbench, you won't hit your knees against the drawer pulls. You can drill the holes after assembling the drawers, but it's a lot easier to do this before the drawers go together.

1. Use a combination square to locate and mark a point centered across the width of the drawer and ¼" down from the top. This is the centerpoint for the drawer pull hole. Use a 1⅛" Forstner or brad-point bit to drill the hole for the drawer pull. Use a piece of scrap under the drawer fronts as you drill to keep the bit from tearing out the underside of the stock, as shown in photo I.

2. Apply glue to the rabbets on the drawer front and back, and then set the sides in place. Drive two 1" brads through each side into the drawer front and back, as shown in photo J. To hide the nails completely, set them with a nail set and fill the holes with putty, as shown in photo K.

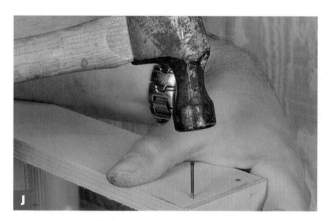

Join the drawers A bead of glue along the rabbet and a few 1" brads or finish nails are all that are needed to join the drawer sides to the front and back.

Pulls without hardware Instead of spending money on hardware, drill a 1⅛"-diameter hole on the top edge of the drawer front and use it as a finger pull for opening and closing the drawers.

Set the nails For a clean look along the edge, set the nails below the surface and fill the hole with natural-colored putty.

3. Center the bottom of the drawer on the underside of the drawer box with the front of the bottom flush with the front of the drawer box. Apply glue and a few brads to secure it in place, as shown in photo L.

4. Install the drawer to test the fit, as shown in photo M. If the fit is tight, trim the bottom with a small block plane. A little wax on the edges of the bottom will keep the action smooth. Repeat these steps for each drawer.

Finish off the drawer **Center the bottom on the drawer. Yellow glue and a few finish nails or smaller brads secure the bottom to the drawer box.**

Test the fit **Once the drawers are together, slide them into the case. If they don't slide smoothly, plane the bottoms until they do.**

Install the case of drawers

The case seen here is sized to fit the workbench built on pp. 28–55, but you can build a similar design to go in any number of places. If you did build it for your bench, remove the lower shelf from the bench, put the case of drawers in place, and sink a few drywall screws through the bottom of the case of drawers into the lower stretchers on the bench, as shown in photo N. Then slide all of the drawers into place.

Install the case **If your box of drawers is headed for your workbench, set the case in place and drive a few drywall screws into the lower stretcher of the bench.**

> **WORK SMART**
>
> If your drawers are a bit snug in the openings, use a block plane to trim either the width of the drawer bottom or its thickness, depending on which part is sticking.

Two-Door Storage Cabinet

Shelving is great—it puts everything in sight and keeps it off the workbench—but a shelving unit with doors is even better. It allows you to store tools and supplies out of sight and keeps them from getting dusty as you work in the shop. While building this project, you'll learn how to add a face frame and doors, as well as how to outfit a cabinet for adjustable shelves. For more simple open shelving units, you can build the same unit without doors. The face frame can also be left off.

TOOLS

- Combination square
- Tape measure or folding rule
- tablesaw
- Biscuit joiner
- Mallet
- Hammer
- Two clamps, at least 40" long
- Drill
- ¼" brad-point drill bit
- Drill press or drilling guide
- Handsaw
- Two sawhorses
- Dado set
- Marking knife
- Marking gauge
- 1" chisel
- Pencil
- A few dimes
- Level

MATERIALS

Quantity	Part	Actual Size	What to Buy
2	Sides	¾" x 8¼" x 32"	½ sheet of ¾" plywood
1	Top	¾" x 8¼" x 27½"	
1	Bottom	¾" x 8¼" x 27½"	
1	Back	¼" x 28" x 31"	
2	Face frame verticals	¾" x 1⅞" x 32"	Maple, poplar, or a similar hardwood
2	Face frame horizontals	¾" x 2½" x 25⅛"	Hardwood
2	Door	¾" x 27⅛" x 12½"	
4	Butt hinges	1½" x 12½"	Brass or steel
8	#20 biscuits		Buy a container full. You'll use them for other projects.
4	#0 biscuits		Buy a container full. You'll use them for other projects.
1	Drilling guide	¾" x 3" x 26"	Plywood
2	Cleats	½" x 3" x 27"	Plywood
2	Shelves	¾" x 7½" x 27¼"	This design has two shelves installed, but you can add more if you wish.
8	Shelf pins	¼" dia. x ¾" long	Cut from ¼" dowel. You can also buy brass or plastic shelf pins.
	Finish nails	1½"	Buy a box so you'll have them on hand.
	Wood screws	#4	Use steel, not brass.
2	Friction catches		Screws for attaching come with the hardware.
1	Small block	¾" x 3" x 1½"	
2	Door pulls		
	Misc.		Yellow glue

Two-Door Storage Cabinet

A face frame, simple plywood doors, and adjustable shelves make this cabinet a versatile storage spot for items you'd rather keep out of sight and away from dust.

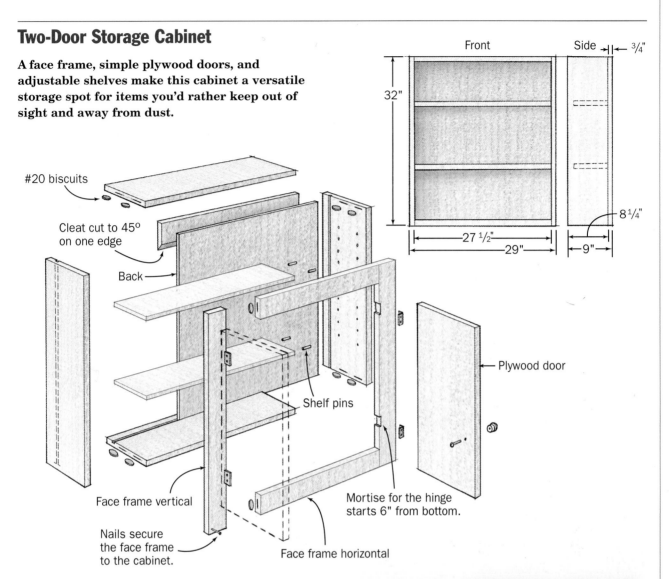

#20 biscuits

Cleat cut to 45°
on one edge

Back

Shelf pins

Face frame vertical

Nails secure
the face frame
to the cabinet.

Face frame horizontal

Mortise for the hinge
starts 6" from bottom.

Plywood door

Front   Side   3/4"

32"

27 1/2"

29"

9"

8 1/4"

Buying Materials

Chances are, if you've built another project in this book, you have enough scrap ¾" plywood on hand to build the basic cabinet and the doors. Maple was used for the face frame shown here, but poplar or pine would work as well. Just choose a wood that matches the color of the plywood. You can find the lumber as well as the hinges, friction catches, and wooden pulls at any home center. Inexpensive hardware works fine for shop projects.

A

Store it out of sight Whether you're making a small cabinet for storing finishing supplies or a larger version for power tools, the building methods are the same.

Building the Basic Case

The basic case is built with ¾" plywood that is grooved to accept the back and biscuited together at the corners. You'll start by cutting all the stock to size and then cutting the joinery. Then, before you assemble the case, you'll drill the sides to accept shelf pins. This unit is designed to handle adjustable shelves, but if you'd prefer the shelves to be fixed, you can simply biscuit or nail them in place. If you're making open shelving, those are the only steps to make a shelving unit, but adding a face frame and doors will help keep out the dust. You can even install a lock on the doors.

Cut to size

1. Cut all the case pieces to size (see the drawing on p. 137) at the tablesaw or with a circular saw and cutting guide.

2. Before assembling anything, cut ¼" grooves in the top, bottom, and sides to accept the back of the cabinet, as shown in photo A. You can either use a dado set on the tablesaw or take two passes using a single blade. Inset the groove ½" from the back of the cabinet so that you'll be able to add the cleat later.

3. Trim the back of the cabinet to size. Remember that it needs to extend into the grooves at the back of the cabinet.

4. Cut the two cleats to size. Then cut the edge of each at a 45° angle. For more on this technique, see "Skill Builder: Hanging with a Cleat System" on pp. 148–149.

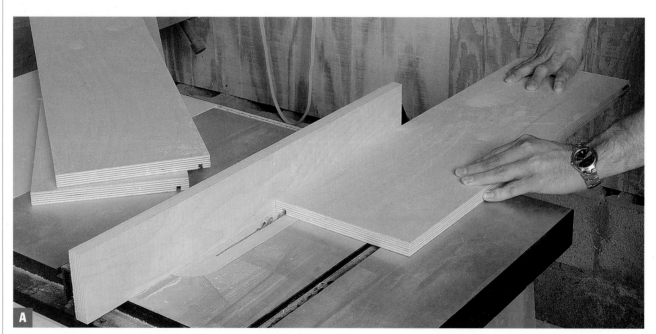

A

Groove for the back With the top, bottom, and sides cut to size, cut grooves to house the back of the cabinet. You can use either a dado set or take two passes with a single blade.

Cut the joinery for the case

1. Lay all the parts out on the bench and use a cabinetmaker's triangle (see "The Cabinetmaker's Triangle" on p. 63) to mark the top, bottom, and sides.

2. Butt the ends of the sides against the bench stop or another 90° stop. Set your biscuit joiner to cut #20 biscuits. Mark out the biscuit locations or, since there are just a few slots to cut, save time and align the edge of the biscuit joiner with the edge of the case pieces and plunge-cut, as shown in photo B.

3. Lay the top and bottom of the case flat on the benchtop. Align the edge of the biscuit joiner with the outer edges of the piece, then plunge-cut, as shown in photo C.

Biscuit the sides Brace the biscuit joiner against a 90° stop and align the edge of the machine with the edge of the cabinet, then plunge to cut a slot for a #20 biscuit.

Cut slots in the ends Lay the top and bottom flat on the bench, align the biscuit joiner with the edge of the piece, and plunge to make the cut.

Drilling Holes and Making Shelf Pins

Making adjustable shelves may sound complicated, but it's not. In many cases, it's a lot easier than building fixed shelves. It's a good idea to have adjustable shelves in the shop to accommodate your tools and supplies as they grow and change. For adjustable shelves, all you need to do is drill holes in the sides of a case and insert shelf pins to support the shelves. To raise or lower a shelf, you simply move the shelf pins to another set of holes.

You can buy drilling guides, but making your own offers much more flexibility. I keep a number of drilling guides on hand around

D

E

Make the guide Use either a drilling guide or a drill press to drill 90° holes spaced 1½" apart and centered on the guide.

Drill for the shelves Clamp the guide in place against the edge of the case side. Take care not to drill all the way through the side of the cabinet.

the shop—some have holes aligned at every inch, others at 2" intervals. I also make custom guides for specific projects.

You can buy brass or plastic shelf pins at hardware stores, but using lengths of dowels is both cheaper and better looking.

1. To make the drilling guide, cut a length of ¾" plywood to 3" x 26". Use a combination square to locate the centerpoint across the width of the board, then mark out holes at 1½" intervals. You can drill the ¼" holes using either a drill press, as shown in photo D or a drilling guide set to 90°.

2. To use the guide, align it with the bottom and side of a side case piece, then clamp it in place.

3. Before drilling, put tape on the drill bit at 1⅛" so you will not drill deeper than that. This amount allows for the thickness of the guide so you'll get a ⅜"-deep hole in the side. It will also prevent you from drilling through the side of the cabinet.

4. With the tape in place, drill the holes, as shown in photo E. Then clamp the guide to the other side of the case piece and repeat the process. Repeat again for the opposite case piece to get two rows of holes there. To secure a shelf, you'll need a total of four rows of holes.

5. To make the shelf pins, use a handsaw to cut pins to ¾" long. Test-fit the pins to make sure they fit well, as shown in photo F.

F

Insert the shelf pins Once the cabinet is assembled, insert shelf pins into the holes to anchor the shelves.

Assemble the case

1. Before gluing up the cabinet, dry-fit the parts without any glue to make sure you won't encounter any surprises during the final assembly. Then disassemble.

2. Lay one of the sides across two sawhorses or let it hang off either side of the workbench. Glue the biscuits into their slots and add glue to the biscuits and edges. Then set the top and bottom in place, as shown in photo G.

3. Put a small bead of glue in each of the grooves on the back of the cabinet and slide the back into place, as shown in photo H.

4. Glue biscuits into the ends of the upright top and bottom. Add a little glue to the biscuits and a small bead of glue on the plywood edges. Set the other side in place, as shown in photo I.

Insert the back **Add just a few drops of glue into each of the grooves.**

Set the ends in place **With one side of the cabinet laying across sawhorses, add glue and biscuits, then set the top and bottom in place.**

Secure the other side **Put the biscuits into place, then set the other side onto the assembly.**

WORK SMART

When possible, glue up cabinets with the back in place. Because the back is cut perfectly square, your cabinet should go together that way as well.

What You'll Need

- **1" chisel**
- **Marking gauge**
- **Mallet**
- **Combination square**
- **Marking knife**
- **Pencil**

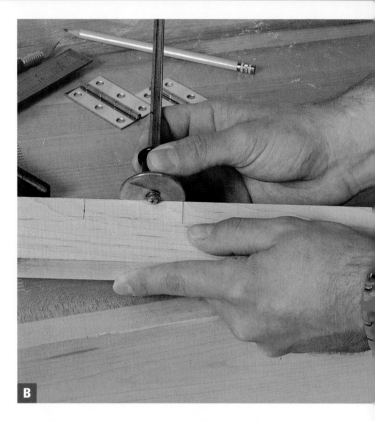

B

There are numerous ways to cut mortises—with handheld routers, on router tables, or with specially designed mortising machines. But mortises for hinges are so shallow and small that using a router usually isn't worth the trouble because you have to fine-tune the cut with a chisel anyway. Learning to cut a mortise by hand teaches you to mark out for a hinge and shows you which measurements are critical. It's also a good way to improve your techniques with a chisel.

The method described here walks you through the steps in cutting a mortise for a butt hinge, but it comes in handy for mortising to fit other pieces of hardware around the shop.

A

1. Set the hinge in place on the stock you'll be mortising. Hold the hinge steady and flush to the edge, then mark out the hinge using a marking knife, as shown in photo A.

2. Set a marking gauge just shy of half the width of the hinge barrel, then mark a line on both sides of the vertical frame member. The marking gauge may want to follow the grain of the wood, so take care to keep the guide pressed tightly against the side of the stock, as shown in photo B.

3. At the knife mark, place a chisel bevel-edge down. Moving down the width of the mortise, give the chisel light taps with a mallet to make a series of small cuts about ⅛" apart, as shown in photo C. Be sure not to cut below the mark on the edge of the stock.

4. With the bevel side of the chisel facing up, pare across the mortise until you reach the depth marked on the sides, as shown in photo D. You'll need to chop downward occasionally to re-establish the knifed lines marking the length of the hinge.

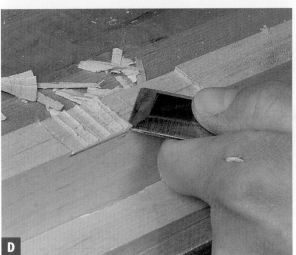

Clamp it up A few clamps should pull the joints closed.

Check for square Measure the diagonals across both corners. If the case is square, you'll get equal measurements for both diagonals. If not, adjust the clamps or add another across the long diagonal.

5. Apply clamps spanning from side to side to pull all the joints closed, as shown in photo J. You should see a small bead of glue bleed out of the joints. You can wipe it off now, but I find it easiest to remove excess glue with a chisel after it cures for about 30 minutes.

6. To ensure that the assembly has gone together square, use a tape to measure the diagonals from corner to corner, as shown in photo K. If the measurements are the same, the assembly is square; if not, adjust the clamps or add another one from corner to corner and tighten until the measurements are the same.

Adding a Face Frame and Doors

Whether you're building freestanding bookcases or built-in cabinetry, building and installing face frames is a task you'll encounter repeatedly. I've tried various methods for installing face frames—and there are almost as many methods as there are cabinetmakers—but the one outlined here is the easiest I've tried. I always use hardwoods for face frames, and I use #0 biscuits to ensure that all the front faces are flush to one another. Some people assemble the frames before they go on the case, but I find it easier to glue and nail the parts into place, one at a time, on the cabinet itself.

Make the face frame

1. Measure and mark a length of stock (at least 3½" wide) to the height of the cabinet. On the tablesaw, cut the stock to length, and then rip that piece into two pieces 1⅞" wide. These are the face frame verticals.

2. On the tablesaw, rip two other lengths of stock to 2½" wide. These will be the face frame horizontals.

3. Clamp the two vertical frame pieces flush to the edge of one side of the cabinet, then hold the horizontals in place and mark them to length, as shown in photo L. Crosscut the horizontals to length using a miter gauge on your tablesaw.

4. Set the face frame members flat on the benchtop or clamp them in place on the front of the cabinet, then mark centerlines for the biscuit slots, as shown in photo M.

5. Once the centerlines are marked, lay the frame parts flat on your bench and clamp them. Set the biscuit joiner for #0 biscuits and plunge to make the cut, as shown in photo M.

6. If you're adding doors to the case, it's easier to mortise for the hinges before you install the face frame. Measure and mark

Measure the frame members With the two vertical pieces of the face frame cut to length and width, clamp them flush to one side, then hold the horizontal frame pieces in place and mark for length.

Mark for biscuits With the frame members held in place, mark out centerlines for #0 biscuits.

N

Biscuit the frame With the frame members flat on the bench, set the biscuit joiner for #0 biscuit slots, then plunge to make the cut.

O

Nail on the frame Start applying the face frame by nailing on one of the vertical members. Add a biscuit and glue before attaching the horizontals.

the mortise locations with a marking gauge and marking knife. It's easiest to cut shallow mortises like these by hand with a chisel. For more on this technique, see "Skill Builder: Mortising for Hinges by Hand" on pp. 142–143. If you decide to add doors later, remove the cabinet from the wall and lay it on its side on the benchtop to cut the mortises.

7. Once the mortises are cut, you're ready to glue and nail the face frame in place. Start by nailing and gluing on one vertical frame piece, then add a biscuit and glue and attach one of the horizontal frame pieces, as shown in photo O. Apply glue along the edge of the cabinet, and add a few nails to hold the horizontal in place.

Make the doors

The doors on this cabinet are nothing more than two pieces of plywood, but when they're closed, you don't see any of the raw edges.

1. Measure and mark two pieces of ¾" plywood to fit inside the face frame. Aim for a gap on all sides of ¹⁄₁₆" (about the thickness of a dime). Cut the pieces on the tablesaw.

2. With the mortises cut in the face frame, you need to transfer the mortise locations to the doors, as shown in photo P. Set each door in place in the opening, using a few dimes as spacers to help you position it correctly. Mark

P

Mark mortises on the door Use a few dimes to shim the door into place, then transfer the mortise location from the face frame to the door. Cut the mortise just as you did on the frame.

the mortise locations directly off the mortises in the face frame and mark the depth using a marking gauge.

3. Use a 1" chisel to cut the mortises in the door, and follow the same methods you used for cutting the mortises in the face frames (see "Skill Builder: Mortising for Hinges by Hand" at on pp. 142–143).

Hang the doors

1. Attach the hinges to the mortises in the doors, as shown in photo Q. Locate the center of the hinge barrel about $\frac{1}{32}$" proud of the front of the door. Predrill the hole for the center screw, then install the screw. Make sure the inside edge of the hinge is parallel to the inside edge of the door before predrilling the holes for and installing the other screws.

2. With the hinges installed on the doors, set them in place on the cabinet. Again, locate the center of the barrel about $\frac{1}{32}$" proud of the front of the door. Predrill and install only the center screw on each hinge.

3. With only one screw in each hinge, close the cabinet door and make sure it closes with

the door flush to the face frame. If not, remove the screw in the hinge, make the necessary adjustments, and then install a screw in one of the other holes to test again. Once the door closes flush to the frame, install all of the screws, as shown in photo R.

R

Hang the door **Align the hinges into the mortises on the frame, then screw a single screw in place. If the door doesn't close flush, remove the screw and start over. Don't add additional screws until you see that the door closes flush.**

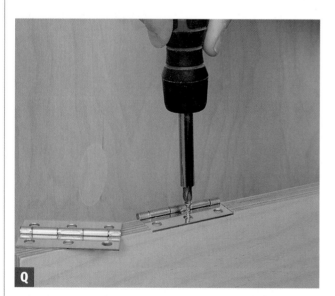

Q

Attach the hinge to the door **Before hanging the door, attach the hinge to the door with screws.**

> ## WORK SMART
>
> When installing brass hinges—or any hardware that comes with brass screws—replace the brass screws with steel ones, because the brass ones are likely to break. If you prefer the look of brass screws, remove the steel ones and replace them one at a time after the steel ones have established the hole.

Adding the Finishing Touches

The cleat system used to secure this cabinet is as simple as it gets, but it's also the strongest way I know of to install a cabinet on a wall. After the cleat is installed on the back of the cabinet, you'll need only to add pulls to the doors and a friction catch to keep the doors closed. Once the cabinet is on the wall, you're ready to install the shelves and clean up shop.

1. Cut and install the cleats on the back of the cabinet and on the wall (see "Skill Builder: Hanging with a Cleat System" on pp. 148–149).

2. To add the friction catch, flip the cabinet upside down, then glue and clamp a small block flush with the face frame to the top of the inside of the cabinet.

3. Attach the female end of one catch to the small block about ⅛" in from the top edge of the door, as shown in photo S.

Install the shelves **With the shelf pins in place, the shelves simply rest upon them.**

Install a door catch **Friction catches keep the doors closed. Glue a block to the frame. Screw one part of the catch on the block, then the other on the door.**

4. With one door closed and the other open, position the catch on the inside of the closed door so that it is in line with the female end of the catch on the small block when the door is closed flush, and mark the location. If you center the screws in the holes on the catch, they leave a little room for adjustment after they're installed. Repeat steps 3 and 4 for the other door's friction catch.

5. To install the door pulls, predrill holes about 8" up from the bottom of the door and about 2" in from the edge. Then set the screws in place from inside the doors and thread the pulls onto them.

6. Hang the cabinet on the wall. Add the shelf pins and put in the shelves, as shown in photo T. Now you're ready to load up the cabinet with tools and supplies.

What You'll Need

- **Tablesaw**
- **½" plywood, 6" x 27"**
- **Screws**
- **Level**

The cleat system seen here has been around for ages, and everyone seems to have a different name for it. I've often heard it called a French cleat, but I once heard a woodworker refer to it as an Indian cleat. "It depends," he told me, "on how you viewed that war."

Either way, it's a simple method that works beautifully. You cut one piece of stock in half at a 45° angle, then mount one piece on the back of the cabinet and anchor the other to the wall. To hang the cabinet, you just lift the cleat of the cabinet over the cleat on the wall, then lower it on to the other. The two cleats lock together, holding the cabinet snug to the wall.

1. Cut a length of stock 6" wide and as long as the piece you're hanging. Then set your tablesaw to cut at 45° and cut down the center to create two cleats, as shown in photo A.

2. Attach one cleat to the cabinet using glue and drywall screws. Make sure the angled edge is facing down and that the long, full side of the stock is facing the wall, as shown in photo B.

3. Attach the other cleat to the wall, with the shorter angled side against the wall, pointing up. Attach one screw, adjust the cleat so it's level, and then add the other

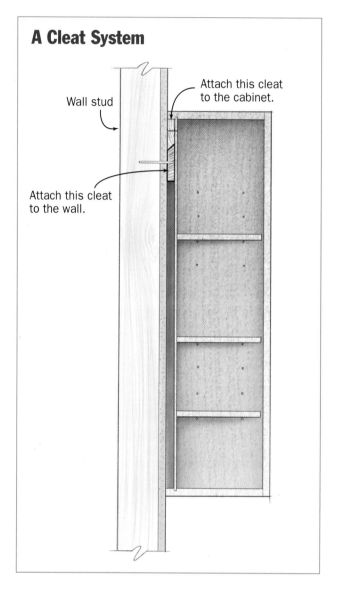

A Cleat System

Wall stud

Attach this cleat to the cabinet.

Attach this cleat to the wall.

screws, as shown in photo C. Make sure that at least one screw goes into a wall stud. On larger cabinets or cabinets holding a lot of weight, you'll need more than one screw in a wall stud.

4. To hang the cabinet, lift it to the wall, raise the cleat of the cabinet over the cleat on the wall, then lower the cabinet into place. The two cleats lock together and secure the cabinet in place.

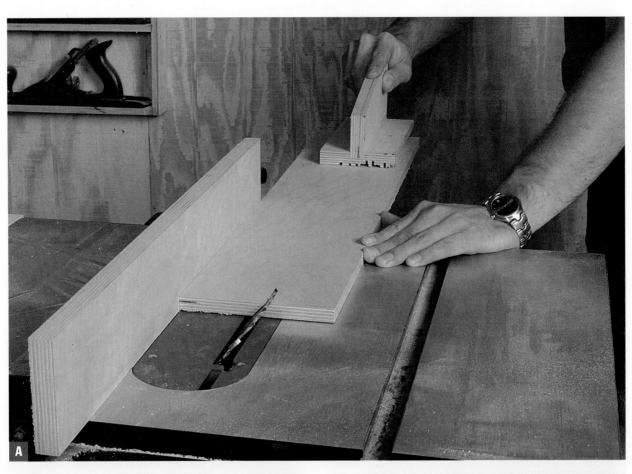

A Better Pegboard

A place for everything Keep your essential tool set within reach and in easy view.

If you walk the aisles of any home center, you'll find many variations on the traditional pegboard. And while some of them are slight improvements over the old-fashioned version, most are expensive and cumbersome to use. For less money and about the same amount of time it takes to arrange tools on a pegboard, you can design and build a personalized tool board. It will look attractive and work great. The tool board shown here holds most of the hand tools used throughout this book and will hang on the wall just above your workbench.

MATERIALS

Quantity	Part	Actual Size	What to Buy
1	Back	½" x 24½" x 35"	About a ½ sheet of plywood—½" x 36" x 36"—is enough for the project.
1	Shelf	½" x 3" x 35"	Use the extra from the plywood for the tool board.
	Extra stock for tool holders	Various	You can use any offcuts from ½" plywood or hardwood.
	Pegs	¼" dia., about 12" long	Cut the pegs from a ¼"-dia. dowel.
	Flat magnets	¾" dia.	The number you need depends on your tool collection.
2	Cleats	½" x 3" x 35"	
1 tube	5-minute epoxy		Buy the plunger-type dispenser, which has two chambers.
1 box	Drywall screws	⅞" long	
1 box	Finish nails	1¼"	
	Brads		You may want some on hand in case you need to reinforce the glue joints.
2	Back spacer blocks	½" x 3" x 3"	
	Misc.		Yellow glue

A Custom Tool Board

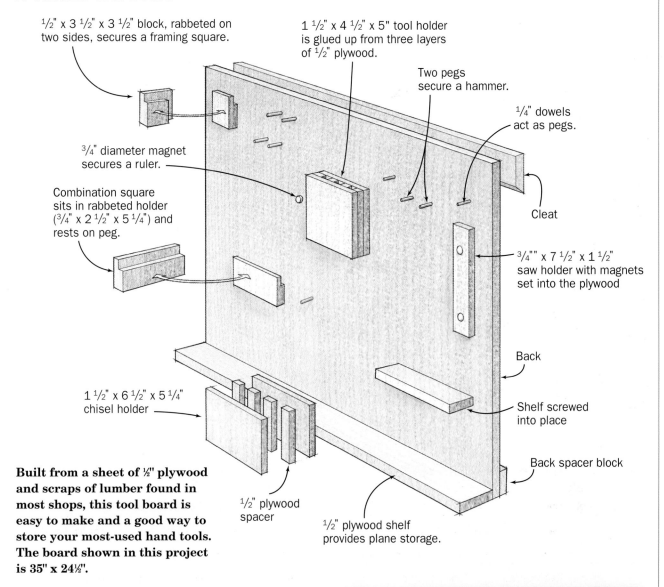

$\frac{1}{2}$" x 3 $\frac{1}{2}$" x 3 $\frac{1}{2}$" block, rabbeted on two sides, secures a framing square.

1 $\frac{1}{2}$" x 4 $\frac{1}{2}$" x 5" tool holder is glued up from three layers of $\frac{1}{2}$" plywood.

Two pegs secure a hammer.

$\frac{1}{4}$" dowels act as pegs.

$\frac{3}{4}$" diameter magnet secures a ruler.

Combination square sits in rabbeted holder ($\frac{3}{4}$" x 2 $\frac{1}{2}$" x 5 $\frac{1}{4}$") and rests on peg.

Cleat

$\frac{3}{4}$"" x 7 $\frac{1}{2}$" x 1 $\frac{1}{2}$" saw holder with magnets set into the plywood

Back

1 $\frac{1}{2}$" x 6 $\frac{1}{2}$" x 5 $\frac{1}{4}$" chisel holder

Shelf screwed into place

Back spacer block

Built from a sheet of ½" plywood and scraps of lumber found in most shops, this tool board is easy to make and a good way to store your most-used hand tools. The board shown in this project is 35" x 24½".

$\frac{1}{2}$" plywood spacer

$\frac{1}{2}$" plywood shelf provides plane storage.

Buying Materials

This entire project can be built from a single piece of ½" plywood about 3' x 3'. You'll also want to pick up a dispenser of 5-minute epoxy, a few ¾"-diameter flat magnets, and a length of ¼" dowel. All of these supplies should be available at your local home center.

TOOLS

- ■ **Combination square**
- ■ **Tape measure or folding rule**
- ■ **Tablesaw with high fence**
- ■ **5-minute epoxy**
- ■ **Yellow glue**
- ■ **Mallet or hammer**
- ■ **Level**
- ■ **Drill**
- ■ **¾" Forstner bit**
- ■ **¼" brad-point bit**
- ■ **Countersink bit**

Determining Your Needs

efore you build the tool board, you need to decide what tools will go on the board. For my cabinet, I chose the hand tools I reach for most often: a set of four chisels, a framing square, a block plane and two longer planes, an awl, a bevel gauge, a marking gauge, a small gent's saw, a hammer, a rubber mallet, a folding rule, a tri-square, and a combination square. If you've got other tools you find yourself reaching for often, add them to the mix—it's likely that one of the holder designs described here can be adapted to handle them.

Gather up the tools you want to store on the tool board. Spread them out on a flat surface and arrange them the way you want them on the tool board. (It may help to read through all of the small projects for the tool board to get ideas for where to put each tool.)

WORK SMART

If you plan to buy more tools in the near future, leave extra room on your tool board so you'll be able to add other holders later.

As a rule, it's easiest to start with the larger tools. And remember that when you're placing tools like chisels that will have to be pulled upward in order to be removed from the tool board, you'll need to make sure there's plenty of clearance above the tools. Once you're satisfied with the arrangement of tools, measure the space they take up, as shown in photo A, and cut your board to size. (The board shown in this project is 35" x 24½".)

A

Choose your favorites **Whatever tools you find yourself reaching for most often should be collected and arranged to determine the size of the board you need. When you find a working arrangement, measure the length and width and cut a board to size.**

Building a tool board is just a step away from building your own custom tool cabinet.

The tool cabinet seen here started out as a tool board. In time, I added a rabbeted box around the board and eventually decided that I needed to add more storage—so on went the doors. The doors are nothing more than boxes hinged to the center box using long continuous hinges. These are all skills you've learned from the projects in this book, and you can apply them here if you'd like. It's a day's work, but it's a rewarding day.

Adding a Shelf for Handplanes

Small block planes need only a small shelf glued and screwed onto the tool board. Be sure to predrill and countersink the holes for the screws so that you won't split the shelf.

Larger handplanes, like the #4 and #5 seen here, require a large shelf screwed to the bottom of the tool board.

1. Measure the width of the largest plane, then set the rip fence on your tablesaw for a cut about ¼" wider than the plane. Cut a piece of plywood to that width.

2. Cut the shelf to the length of the tool board.

3. Apply yellow glue to the shelf, then screw it in place through the back of the tool board using drywall screws, as shown in photo B. Be sure to predrill and countersink the screw holes so that there's no risk of splitting the shelf when you drive the screws home.

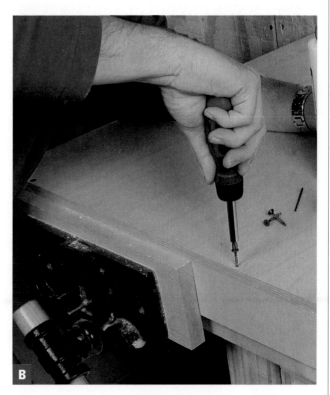

Start with a shelf Large handplanes are easily stored on a simple shelf screwed to the bottom of the tool board.

Making a Chisel Holder

Even if the bulk of your work relies on using power tools, a set of four chisels—¼", ½", ¾", and 1"—are a must for any workshop. To hang them on a tool board, build a simple block that holds them much in the same way kitchen knives are held in a wooden block. To make the block, you'll need just a few scraps of ½" plywood. The chisel block rests on the handplane shelf, so there's no reason to cap the bottom of it, but blocks for other tools can be capped to keep the tools from sliding through the openings, as shown in photo C. You can make similar holders to handle your awl, bevel gauge, and marking gauge.

1. Lay out your chisels on a scrap of plywood. Arrange them so that the blades don't extend past the edge of the plywood and there's enough space around the handles so that they won't bump into each other. For my chisels, I needed ¾"-wide spacers between the chisels to keep the handles from bumping. Measure the overall size you'll need for the block based on how many chisels you have and the size and number of spacers. You'll use spacers as the sides of the holder, so be sure to include those in your measurements.

2. Using the tablesaw, cut two pieces of ½" plywood to size to make up the front and back of the holder. Cut the ½"-thick plywood spacers to the width you determined in step 1. Then trim the spacers to the height of the chisel holder.

5-MINUTE EPOXY: THE QUICK FIX

For some reason, I did years of woodworking before I bought my first $2 dispenser of 5-minute epoxy. Little did I know how many times it would come in handy. You can use 5-minute epoxy any time you want to attach something permanently but don't have time to wait for yellow glue to dry, or in situations where getting a clamp in place is challenging.

Mixing up a batch of 5-minute epoxy is quick and easy. Epoxy is a two-part adhesive, meaning that the chemical reaction that causes it to harden doesn't begin until the two parts are mixed together. You can buy it in dispensers with a plunger that pushes out equal parts of each component so there's no measuring. Simply squirt out what you need and mix the two together until they're a solid color. Once the mix is consistent, spread it on the parts you want to adhere and either use a clamp or a weight to hold the parts while the epoxy cures. The glue cures in—you guessed it—about 5 minutes.

Cap the bottom This holder is capped at the bottom so the tools won't slide out.

Make a custom chisel holder Glue spacers in place between the blades of the chisels.

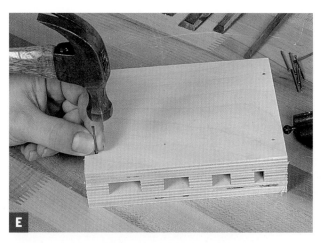

Nail on the top Once the spacers are in place, nail the front board in place over them.

Test it out Before you attach the chisel holder to the tool board, give it a test run and make sure all the chisels slide easily into place.

3. Position the first spacer on the back of the box and glue it into place with yellow glue. You can add a small brad or two, if necessary, to keep it in place. With the first spacer in place, lay the first chisel in place, then position the second spacer and glue it in place. Continue until all the chisels and spacers are in place, as shown in photo D.

4. Remove the chisels and place the front of the box on the spacers. Glue it on and add 1¼" nails at each corner to hold the assembly together, as shown in photo E.

5. Test-fit your chisels to make sure they don't come through the bottom of the holder and that they fit properly, as shown in photo F. If they fit well, you're ready to attach the holder to the tool board. Place the holder on the tool-board shelf—making sure there's still room for the handplanes—and then glue it in place. You can use yellow glue and clamps to secure it, or mix up a batch of 5-minute epoxy (see "5-Minute Epoxy: The Quick Fix" on the facing page) and set it in place with a little weight on top.

Adding a Framing Square

You'll find yourself reaching for a framing square quite often, so it's best to keep one close at hand. Adding one to your tool board takes nothing but a scrap of plywood or hardwood at least 8" square.

1. Install a high fence on your tablesaw and use a single blade to cut a rabbet just over ⅛" wide and about ¾" deep. Use a scrap of wood at least 8" square. Cut rabbets in two adjacent edges, keeping the stock face flat against the high fence.

2. Cut the stock down to a 3" x 3" square at your tablesaw. Do not cut off the rabbeted ends.

3. Set the block in place on the tool board and make sure the thickness of the rabbet is sufficient to allow the framing square to slide in and out easily. Then locate the block

so that it rests square to two edges of the tool board and mark out the block location, as shown in photo G.

4. Use 5-minute epoxy to secure the block to the tool board and clamp it in place for just a few minutes. Use the epoxy sparingly so that none of it squeezes out into the rabbet and blocks the framing square from sliding into place.

Add a framing square Mark the location for the framing square block, then glue it into place on the tool board.

Hanging Tools Using Magnets

Some people like to hang the bulk of their tools from magnets—either small ¾"-diameter magnets like those used here or longer flat strips of magnets designed to hold chisels and the like. On this tool board, I used magnets for holding up small rulers and the gent's saw. The weight of the saw requires two magnets to secure it in place. To allow room for the saw handle, the magnets are mounted on a block of ¾" plywood, and then the block is mounted onto the tool board. The setup works nicely for both these tools, but a similar arrangement works well to secure any metal tool. Mounting a round magnet takes only a few minutes.

Set the magnet in place Mix a batch of 5-minute epoxy and apply it inside the drilled hole, then drop the magnet in place.

1. Locate the tool on the tool board and mark out a centerpoint for the magnet location.

2. Use a ¾" Forstner bit to drill a hole centered on your mark, as shown in photo H. Make sure your magnet fits in the hole either flush or just a bit proud.

3. Mix up a small batch of 5-minute epoxy, dab just a bit of it into the hole, and then set the magnet in place, as shown in photo I. If the fit is tight, clamping usually isn't necessary. Lay the board on its back until the glue dries.

Drill holes for the magnet Take care not to drill too deep—the magnet should sit just proud of the face of the board.

> ### WORK SMART
>
> Sometimes the best way to hang a tool is by using a combination of the methods discussed in this project. For the combination square, I use both a peg and a rabbeted block to secure the tool. With this arrangement, I don't have to move the blade of the combination square every time I want to hang the tool.

Dowels Make Quick Pegs

You can hang many tools from pegs: hammers, mallets, and squares, to name just a few, as shown in photo J. If your tools change in the future, you can trim the pegs flush with a saw and chisel to get rid of old pegs, or drive new ones into place.

1. Locate your tools on the board and mark the peg locations. Measure the length you need for each peg. Remember, you want the tools to rest flush against the tool board, so hold the tool against the board to use as a reference when measuring the peg length.

2. Use a ¼" brad-point bit to drill about ⅜" deep into the tool board. Drill at a slightly upturned angle of about 5° so that when the peg is inserted it will tilt up a bit. You could measure the angle with a bevel gauge or tri-square, but eyeballing a slight angle is adequate.

3. Cut a length of ¼" dowel to the sizes you need for the pegs. Add a drop of yellow glue to one end of each dowel, put the dowels in the holes, as shown in photo K, then drive them in place with a hammer. Once you hear the tone of the hammer taps change, your peg has hit the bottom of the hole, so stop hammering. Otherwise, you risk breaking through the back of the tool board.

Two pegs hold a hammer in place The hammer hangs flat against the board, and it will be in easy reach when the board is hung.

Use pegs to hold tools Lengths of ¼" dowels are glued and hammered into place.

Hanging the Tool Board

Once you've got all the tool holders in place, you just need to cut and add cleats to the back of the tool board and the wall so that you can mount it to the wall. For more on this technique, see "Skill Builder:

Hanging with a Cleat System" on pp. 148–149. Once the tool board goes up, set the tools in place. From now on, you'll always know where they are.

Simple Clamp Rack

The old adage among woodworkers says that you can never have enough clamps. And it's true. For that reason, make sure that you build your clamp rack with a few empty spaces left over for clamps you'll buy in the future. This clamp rack is about as basic as it gets, and it can be used to handle bar clamps of any size, as well as smaller trigger-handle clamps. If you have any pipe clamps—those that are threaded onto black pipe—you'll need to adjust the slots in the rack to ¾" wide. To do that, simply drill holes that are ¾" in diameter instead of ½".

Keep clamps close at hand Building a clamp rack not only gets clamps out of the corner of your shop, but it also keeps them clearly displayed so you can reach for the one you need without shuffling through the whole batch.

Clamp Rack Construction

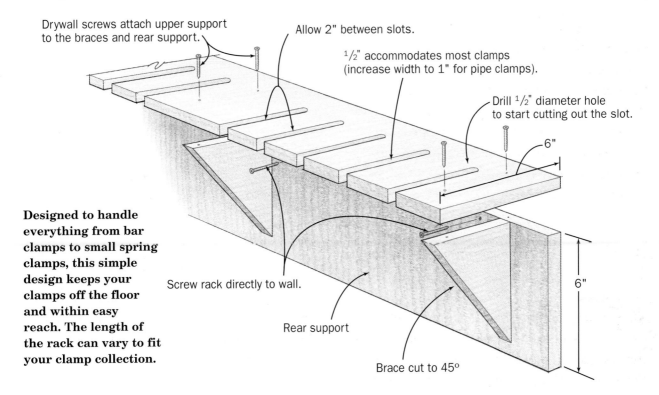

Drywall screws attach upper support to the braces and rear support.

Allow 2" between slots.

½" accommodates most clamps (increase width to 1" for pipe clamps).

Drill ½" diameter hole to start cutting out the slot.

6"

6"

Designed to handle everything from bar clamps to small spring clamps, this simple design keeps your clamps off the floor and within easy reach. The length of the rack can vary to fit your clamp collection.

Screw rack directly to wall.

Rear support

Brace cut to 45°

MATERIALS

Quantity	Part	Actual Size	What to Buy
1	Upper support	¾" x 6". Length varies depending on the number of clamps, but in this project, we made it 32".	Hardwood or plywood
1	Rear support	¾" x 6". Length varies depending on the number of clamps, but in this project, we made it 32".	
3	Braces	5¼" x 5¼"	For safety, you'll need to cut them from longer stock—at least 18" long.
	Scrap board	About the length of the upper support.	
1 box	Drywall screws	1½"	
	Misc.		Yellow glue

TOOLS

- Combination square
- Tape measure or folding rule
- Tablesaw with high fence and miter gauge
- Drill
- ½" or ¾" drill bit
- Level to use when hanging the rack

Buying Materials

Chances are, you have all the lumber you need to make this simple clamp rack lying around in your scrap pile. You'll need only two pieces of ¾" plywood about 32" long and 6" wide, as well as three 5¼"-wide scraps that you will use to make the braces.

1. On the tablesaw, cut the upper and rear supports to 6" wide and the desired length.

2. Locate the centerpoint of the rack on the upper support and mark it as the location for the center brace. Then mark out the location of the two end braces, which should sit flush to the rack's ends. (If you're building a longer rack, locate braces about every 16" to 18" along its length.)

3. Locate and mark centerpoints for all of your clamp slots on the front edge of the upper support, allowing 2" between slots. To help you line up the drill, mark another centerpoint on top of the upper support about 4½" in from the front edge centerpoint.

4. Drill ½"- or ¾"-diameter holes (depending on your clamp size) through the top of the upper support, as shown in photo A. Use a scrap board to back up all the holes so that you won't tear out the bottom edges as you drill through.

5. Use a combination square to mark out lines from each side of the hole out to the front edge, as shown in photo B.

6. Using a high fence on your miter gauge, raise the blade on your tablesaw to cut out the slots you marked in step 5, as shown in photo C. Alternately, you can make the cuts

Drill for the clamps Most clamps can be hung on a ½" opening, but if you use larger pipe clamps, use a ¾" bit to drill the holes.

Lay out slots for the clamps Use a combination square to draw lines perpendicular to the front and aligned with the edges of the drilled holes.

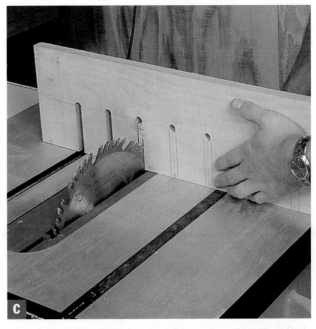

Cut the opening When cutting the slots, use a high fence on the miter gauge and be sure to keep your hands clear of the blade at all times.

D

Cut the brace **Set the miter gauge for a 45° cut and make angled cuts for the braces.**

using a handsaw with the top of the clamp rack secured in the vise on your workbench.

7. Set the miter gauge to 45°. Cut an angle on each end of the piece of 5¼"-wide stock you're using for the braces, as shown in photo D on p. 162. Once the angles are cut, reset the miter gauge to 90° and crosscut the angled ends off. The offcuts are the braces for the rack.

8. To assemble the rack, simply screw the rear edge of the upper support to the rear edge of the rear support, then glue on the braces where you marked them and screw them in, as shown in photo E. Predrill your holes so that you don't risk splitting the plywood.

9. To attach the rack to the wall, you can use a cleat system like the one described in "Skill Builder: Hanging with a Cleat System"

E

Assemble the clamp rack **The upper support is screwed to the rear support, then the braces are glued and screwed to the top and back of the clamp rack.**

on pp. 148–149, but I find it easiest simply to screw it into the studs. As your clamp collection grows, you'll need to build more racks.

Lumber Rack

Lumber Rack Construction

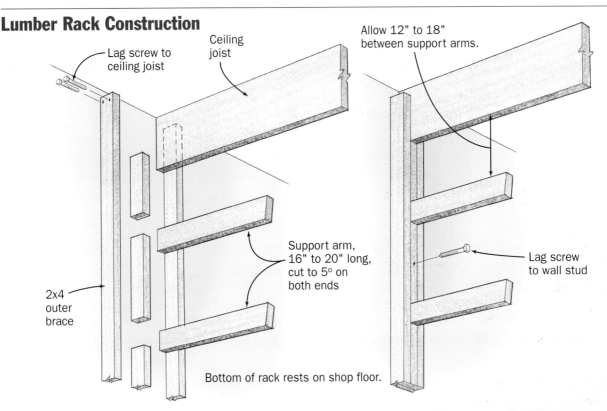

Lag screw to ceiling joist

Ceiling joist

Allow 12" to 18" between support arms.

2x4 outer brace

Support arm, 16" to 20" long, cut to 5° on both ends

Lag screw to wall stud

Bottom of rack rests on shop floor.

Anchored to the wall studs—and tied to the ceiling joists where possible—this lumber rack is strong enough to handle the load of lumber found in a busy shop. Two racks are sufficient for lumber up to 4' long. If you don't have an exposed ceiling joist, use three lag screws instead of one to attach the rack to the wall stud.

Buying Materials

Each column of this lumber rack calls for three 2x4s sized to the ceiling height in your shop. Two column racks are sufficient to hold stock up to about 4' long, but you'll want to add more column racks if you plan to store longer stock. Look for straight boards with as few knots as possible. Besides 2x4s, you'll need a handful of lag screws, as well as a few washers. You can get it all at a home center.

Get lumber out of the way This simply designed lumber rack is as strong as the walls you attach it to. Building one is a good way to get lumber off the floor and to free up workspace.

MATERIALS

Note: The quantities listed here are for one column rack. You will need at least two columns to hold stock, so double the measurements for two columns. You may triple or quadruple the measurements to make more racks to store longer boards.

Quantity	Part	Actual Size	What to Buy
2	Outer braces	2x4. You want them at least as long as your floor-to-ceiling height, or slightly longer.	Construction-grade lumber—either fir or pine—works fine.
Variable	Spacers	2x4s, 12"–18" long	
Variable	Support arms	2x4, 16"–20" long	
	Lag screws	3"	Use this size to attach each of the outer supports to the ceiling joist.
	Lag screws	4"	Use this size to attach the column to the wall stud.
	Washers	1" dia.	You'll need a handful for both the 3" and 4" lag screws.
	Drywall screws	2½" long	
	Misc.		Yellow glue

TOOLS

- ■ Tape measure or folding rule
- ■ Tablesaw
- ■ Miter saw (optional)
- ■ Socket wrench to install the lag screws
- ■ Level

No matter how efficiently you plan your projects, you'll always have stock left over to store, as well as other lumber for future projects. The best way to manage the mess is to build a proper lumber rack.

The lumber rack shown here is a time-tested arrangement that I've seen in many shops. It's made up of inexpensive 2x4 stock that is lag-screwed together. Support arms in between the two outer braces keep the lumber in place against the wall. The whole unit is lag-screwed to the wall studs and, if possible, to the ceiling joists. For the best support, run the 2x4s all the way to the floor, as well. The nice thing about this rack is that you can remove the arms when you don't need to use the rack for storing lumber so the rack then takes up practically no room in the shop. Here are the directions for one column rack.

1. On the tablesaw, cut all the outer braces to length, so that the tops overlap the ceiling joists by about 3" or 4". If you can't access the ceiling joists, cut the outer braces just shy of ceiling height.

2. Cut the spacers on either the miter saw or by using a miter gauge at the tablesaw. Angle both ends of the spacer at 5° in the same direction. Spacers can vary from 12" to 18" long, depending on how much lumber you're planning to store on each arm.

3. Set one outer brace in place on the workbench, and then set your spacers in place. Screw the lower spacer in place using drywall screws. Then set a 2x4 crosswise over the top (to mimic the position of the arm) and another spacer in place on top of the place-

A

Secure the upright to the wall **The top of this lumber rack is lag-screwed to the ceiling joist. About halfway down the column, lag-screw the support to a wall stud. If you can't access the ceiling joists, simply add more screws to the wall stud.**

can't access the ceiling joists, simply attach the rack to the wall stud (see step 6).

5. Use a little glue and some drywall screws to attach the outer brace you just added to the spacers down the length of the support.

6. Predrill for a lag screw through the center spacer and into the wall stud. Then add a washer and screw in the lag screw, as shown in photo A. If you're tied into the ceiling joist, one screw into the wall studs should be sufficient. If not, sink three screws into the wall studs.

7. Use the miter saw or tablesaw to cut support arms to extend from between the spacers. For a cleaner look, angle the ends at 5°.

8. Set the arms in place on the spacers, as shown in photo B, and you're ready to start racking your lumber.

B

Insert the arms **The spacers on this rack are angled up 5° to keep lumber snug to the wall.**

holder arm. Make it a tight fit, then screw the spacer in place. Proceed in this fashion all the way up the outer brace.

4. Once all the spacers are secured to the outer brace, set it in place against the ceiling joist. Set the other outer brace in place on the other side of the ceiling joist. Use lag screws to secure the braces to the ceiling joist. If you

Sources

BENCH DOG TOOLS
3310 5th St. NE
Minneapolis, MN 55418
800-786-8902
www.benchdog.com
A full range of tools and accessories for routers.

BOSCH TOOLS
www.boschtools.com
Handheld and benchtop power tools.

GARRETT WADE
161 Avenue of the Americas
New York, NY 10013
800-221-2942
www.garrettwade.com
Power and hand tools, as well as supplies.

HIGHLAND HARDWARE
1045 North Highland Ave. NE
Atlanta, GA 30306
800-241-6748
www.tools-for-woodworking.com
A wide range of power tools and full range of supplies.

LEE VALLEY TOOLS LTD.
P.O. Box 1780
Ogdensburg, NY 13669-6780
800-513-7885
www.leevalley.com
Power and hand tools, as well as supplies.

LIE-NIELSEN TOOLWORKS
P.O. Box 9
Warren, ME 04864-0009
800-327-2520
www.lie-nielsen.com
High-end hand tools.

McFEELY'S
1620 Wythe Rd.
P.O. Box 11169
Lynchburg, VA 24506-1169
800-443-7937
www.mcfeelys.com
Screws, fasteners, and accessories.

PORTER-CABLE
CORPORATION
4825 Hwy. 45 N.
P.O. Box 2468
Jackson, TN 38302-2468
800-487-8665
www.porter-cable.com
Handheld and benchtop power tools.

ROCKLER WOODWORKING
AND HARDWARE
4365 Willow Dr.
Medina, MN 55340
800-279-4441
www.rockler.com
An array of woodworking tools, especially router accessories.

WOODCRAFT
P.O. Box 1686
Parkersburg, WV 26102-1686
800-225-1153
www.woodcraft.com
The full range of woodworking tools and accessories.

WOODWORKER'S
SUPPLY, INC.
5604 Alameda Pl. NE
Albuquerque, NM 87113
505-821-0500
www.woodworker.com
Power and hand tools, as well as supplies.

Index